Automotive Air-Conditioning Refrigerant Service Guide

Second Edition

by

Philip G. Gott

Published by:
Society of Automotive Engineers, Inc.
400 Commonwealth Drive
Warrendale, PA 15096-0001

Copyright © 1996 Society of Automotive Engineers, Inc.

ISBN 1-56091-521-8

All rights reserved. Printed in the United States of America.

Permission to photocopy for internal or personal use, or the internal or personal use of specific clients, is granted by SAE for libraries and other users registered with the Copyright Clearance Center (CCC), provided that the base fee of $.50 per page is paid directly to CCC, 222 Rosewood Dr., Danvers, MA 01923. Special requests should be addressed to the SAE Publications Group. 1-56091-521-8/96 $.50.

SAE Order No. R-141

Acknowledgement

Thanks to Angelo Patti, Chrysler Corporation; Richard Ligeski, Ford Motor Company; John Elias, General Motors Service Technology Group; and Ward Atkinson, Sun Test Engineering for their help with this second edition.

Table of Contents

1. **Why Use This Service Guide?** 1
   1.1 Purpose 1
   1.2 The Clean Air Act, You, and Your Satisfied Customers 1
   1.3 The Environmental Impact of Some Refrigerants 2
   1.4 Industry Efforts to Solve the Problem 3
   1.5 Legal Requirements 5
   1.6 Proper Procedures and the Right Equipment 5
2. **General Safety and Service Precautions** 7
   2.1 Safety 7
   2.2 Cleanliness 8
   2.3 Check for Leaks First 9
      2.3.1 Background 9
      2.3.2 Leak Detection Equipment 10
      2.3.3 Proper Use of Leak Detection Equipment
             (see SAE Standard J1628): 10
   2.4 Filling 11
3. **Refrigerant and System Properties** 13
   3.1 Cooling Characteristics 13
   3.2 Lubricants 13
   3.3 Contaminants 14
      3.3.1 "Naturally Occurring" Contaminants 14
      3.3.2 Intentionally Introduced Contaminants 15
      3.3.3 Coping With Contaminants 15
   3.4 Why Prevent Mixing of Different Types of
       Refrigerants in Service Equipment? 15
4. **Equipment for the Extraction-only of Refrigerant
   and Equipment for the Recycling of Refrigerant** 17
   4.1 What's the Difference? 17
   4.2 Using Extraction Equipment 18
   4.3 Using Recycling Equipment 19
   4.4 Recycling versus Reclaiming 19
5. **Service Procedure for the Containment
   of Automotive Air-Conditioning Refrigerants** 21
   5.1 Purpose 21
   5.2 Refrigerant Recovery Procedure 21

5.3	Flushing	22
5.4	Recharge/Refilling	23
5.5	Use of a Manifold Gauge Set	23
5.6	Checking Refrigerant for Excess Air	24
5.7	Containers for the Storage of Recycled Refrigerant	25
5.8	Transfer of Refrigerant	25
5.9	Disposal of Empty or Near-Empty Disposable Containers	26

6. Retrofitting CFC-12 (R-12) Mobile Air Conditioning Systems to HFC-134a (R-134a) 27

6.1	Purpose:	27
6.2	Applicability	27
6.3	Retrofit Procedure	27
	6.3.1 Inspection	27
	6.3.2 Check for System Leaks or Other Problems	28

Appendices

Appendix A: Applicable SAE Standards 33

Appendix B: Federal Certification and Record-Keeping Requirements ....

1. Why Use This Service Guide?

1.1 Purpose

The purpose of this book is to help automotive air-conditioning service professionals comply with federal and state certification requirements. To do that this book provides information about:

1.) the damage that R-12 and certain other refrigerants do to the earth's environment,

2.) how to minimize the escape of air-conditioning refrigerants into the atmosphere,

3.) the service equipment available and the importance of complying with SAE standards for both service practices and the selection and use of service equipment, and

4.) retrofitting older air-conditioning systems to the new, environmentally friendly refrigerant, R-134a.

It is assumed that you are or will become familiar with automotive air-conditioning systems and how they are diagnosed and repaired.

1.2 The Clean Air Act, You, and Your Satisfied Customers

Some of the refrigerants used in mobile air-conditioning systems are chlorofluorocarbons with chlorine in their molecular structure. These chlorofluorocarbons are excellent refrigerants and have been selected for use in mobile systems specifically because of their ability to perform well in mobile air conditioners. The most popular of these, R-12, has been used in virtually every passenger car air-conditioning system produced through the 1991 model year. As a family, the chlorofluorocarbons carry the abbreviation "CFC." Within the chemical industry, R-12 is known as CFC-12.

Unfortunately, chlorofluorocarbons do multiple damage to the environment:

1.) The chlorine in the CFCs reacts with and destroys the earth's protective layer of ozone.

2.) CFCs act as a filter by absorbing certain wavelengths of light in a manner similar to that of greenhouse glass, contributing to global warming.

Because of the severe global impact of a depletion in the ozone layer, 68 nations had ratified the "Montreal Protocol" by the fall of 1991. This protocol calls for extensive international efforts to reduce and eventually eliminate the CFCs that damage the ozone layer. (Ozone-damaging CFCs include CFC-11, 12, 113, 114, and 115.)

Recent atmospheric tests have found that the damage to the ozone layer is increasing at a rate much faster than was believed to be the case when the protocol was signed. Therefore, the steps agreed on in the Montreal Protocol are being implemented by various nations at an accelerated pace.

In the United States, the Clean Air Act and follow-up regulations which took effect on November 15, 1991, require that service operations minimize or prevent the release of R-12 and other ozone-damaging refrigerants into the atmosphere. At the same time, a progressive tax has been placed on R-12 to make virgin refrigerant more and more expensive in order to reduce customer demand for this material. R-12 production is being phased down. Ultimately, U.S. production of R-12 will be banned completely after December 31, 1995. Germany, Denmark, and the Netherlands were expected to ban production and use of R-12 by the end of 1994.

This places the burden on the air-conditioning service technician to capture and reuse as much of the refrigerant already in a vehicle's air-conditioning system as possible. This must be done properly so that the customer's air-conditioning system has "like new" performance and durability. Improper capture and reuse of the refrigerant, or the use of the wrong refrigerant, could lead to early system failure and an unhappy customer.

This guide will help you take good care of both the environment and your customer.

1.3 The Environmental Impact of Some Refrigerants

The traditional refrigerants, including R-12, contain chlorine. Upon exposure to sunlight at high altitudes, CFCs break down, releasing the chlorine. The chlorine then attacks and destroys the ozone in the stratosphere. CFCs can remain in the atmosphere for 100 years or more, slowly releasing ozone-damaging chlorine. Therefore, R-12 released today will still be doing environmental damage long after the service technician who released it has retired.

The ozone layer protects the earth's surface from most of the ultraviolet rays of the sun. Some of these rays, ultraviolet "B," are the ones that cause skin cancer and cataracts in humans, and damage crops and many other living organisms. Mankind's release of CFCs over the last 40 or so years has caused very rapid changes in the ozone layer and the level of ultraviolet radiation reaching us. Every 1% decrease in the ozone layer increases the ultraviolet radiation reaching the earth by 1.5 to 2%. This rate of change in the intensity of ultraviolet rays is too fast for living organisms to adapt. For example, if current trends continue unabated, the number of human cataract cases expected by the year 2075 will increase by 18 million. Actions required by the Montreal Protocol to reverse this trend are expected to reduce the projected number of cases significantly.

The increased penetration of ultraviolet rays to the earth's surface also increases the generation of ground-level ozone. While ozone in the stratosphere helps protect the earth, ozone at ground level is a health hazard. When breathed, ozone irritates the air passages in our noses and throats as well as the surface of our lungs.

CFCs also contribute to global warming. Global warming is caused by some gases in the atmosphere which act like the glass in a greenhouse. Greenhouses are warmed by the sun because the glass allows the radiant heat from the sun to enter the greenhouse, but prevents the radiant heat of the earth from leaving. Because they have the same capability as glass to pass or block radiant energy from the sun or the earth, respectively, these gases have become known as "Greenhouse Gases." Warming of the earth due to increases in the amount of these gases in the atmosphere has been called "The Greenhouse Effect."

CFCs are extremely durable in the atmosphere. Some are capable of lasting for over 100 years. Because they are so durable, their concentration can increase substantially over time, accelerating global warming and ozone destruction even further. The fewer CFCs released to the atmosphere, the better.

Mobile air-conditioning systems are by far the largest user of CFCs in the United States. Over 80% of all cars sold in the United States for many years have been fitted with air conditioning. Each system contains at least 1.5 pounds of refrigerant that, if released into the air, will eventually destroy several times its weight in ozone.

Therefore, mobile air-conditioning system production and maintenance have justly attracted a great deal of attention in the fight to preserve the remaining ozone layer.

1.4 Industry Efforts to Solve the Problem

You might ask, "Why not just replace the CFCs in my customers' cars with an environmentally safe refrigerant the next time they need AC service?" Good question. The auto manufacturers and refrigeration industry are working to develop substitute refrigerants and retrofit systems to allow the replacement of R-12 with a more environmentally friendly material. Refrigerants containing reduced amounts of chlorine, the hydrochlorofluorocarbons (HCFCs), have been proposed for this application. These or any other substitute refrigerants are expected to also require the replacement of many pieces of the air-conditioning system. It is not expected that a simple direct or "drop-in" substitute for R-12 will ever be developed.

Under no circumstance must refrigerant other than the one approved by the vehicle or system manufacturer be used in a mobile air-conditioning system. If a refrigerant other than R-12 is to be used in an older system, its use must be accompanied by all of the system changes recommended by the vehicle or system manufacturer. All equipment and instructions necessary to accomplish the recommended changes can be expected to be supplied by the vehicle or system manufacturer.

Retrofit systems are being developed by the vehicle manufacturers to retrofit R-12 systems with R-134a. These systems include new lubricant as well as any required hoses, seals, and dessicant in addition to the less environmentally damaging refrigerant. As will be discussed, mobile air-conditioning systems are designed as a system. Each part must be compatible with all other system components. So, too, will the retrofit systems be complete designs. All of the manufacturer's components must be utilized in order to accomplish a satisfactory retrofit. Partial application of only a few elements of the retrofit system is likely to lead to failure, poor performance, or both. Either case will guarantee an unhappy customer.

Refrigerant manufacturers and the auto industry have developed a replacement for CFCs in new car air-conditioning systems. The refrigerant to be used in new, environmentally friendlier systems is a refrigerant containing hydrogen instead of chlorine. This refrigerant is a member of the hydrofluorocarbon (HFC) refrigerant family. The HFC of choice is HFC-134a, also known as R-134a. Phase-in of R-134a began with the 1992 model year and is expected to be completed in Europe, Japan, and the United States by the 1996 model year.

These environmentally safer refrigerant families carry several different trade names. Because such trade names refer to broad families of refrigerants, they will not be referred to in this guide. It is important that refrigerants be designated by their specific compound name in order to ensure proper air-conditioning system service.

HFCs and HCFCs offer reduced environmental damage in two ways. First, the hydrogen in these refrigerants causes them to be much less stable in the atmosphere than CFCs. Their lifetime in the atmosphere is only 2 to 25 years, 4 to over 50 times shorter than the CFCs. While the HCFCs still contain chlorine, the increased chemical instability of HCFC in the atmosphere causes the chlorine to be dispersed at lower altitudes—below the ozone layer. Second, the HFCs are still greenhouse gases, but much less so. Figure 1 presents the relative environmental damage potentials of CFC-12, HFC-134a, and possible retrofit refrigerants. CFC-11, once commonly used as a flushing agent for mobile air-conditioning systems, is also shown.

Because the HCFCs still contain chlorine, they are considered more as a transition material than a long-term solution to the problem. Some of the refrigerants shown in Figure 1 may be blended together and used in conjunction with approved retrofit components in older systems, for example. However, atmospheric data collected since the 1990 Montreal Protocol was first signed indicates that the ozone problem is more severe than originally believed. This increased concern may disallow HCFCs altogether.

As previously mentioned, it is not possible to just replace harmful CFC refrigerant with an environmentally safer material such as R-134a. Air-conditioning equipment is designed as a system. The refrigerant and its thermodynamic, physical, and chemical properties are a key factor in the overall system design. If you were to just replace R-12 with R-134a, for example, your customers' air-conditioning systems would perform poorly at low speeds such as in city traffic. Eventually the compressor and other system parts would fail due to chemical attack, overpressure, and poor lubrication.

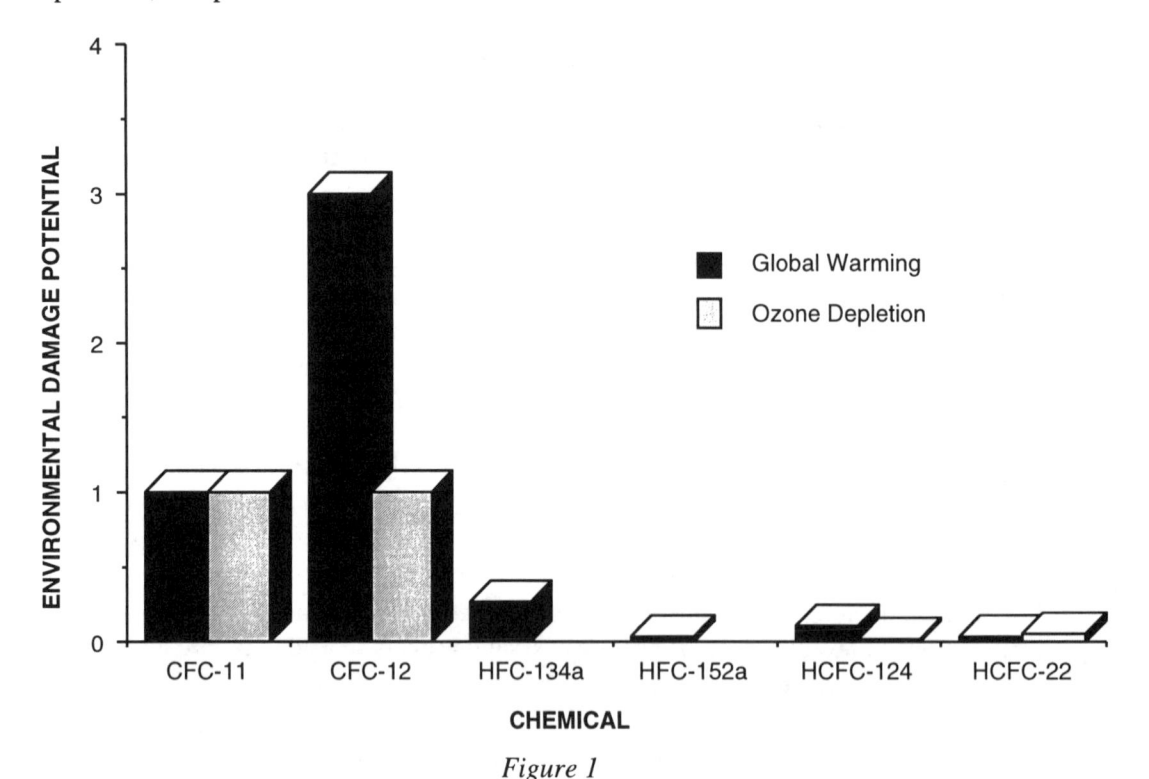

Figure 1

Relative Environmental Damage Potential of Current and Possible Refrigerants and CFC-11, a Flushing Agent

Your best choice is to properly capture and recycle to industry standards any refrigerant that you use. Recycling CFC and HCFC refrigerants was required nationwide by the EPA as of January 1, 1992, although some states required it earlier. The EPA requires the recovery and recycling of HFCs (R-134a) beginning November 15, 1995. Recovery and recycling will minimize the amount of refrigerant released from your service operations and will allow you to provide environmentally sound service while keeping your customers' air-conditioning systems operating satisfactorily.

Since the production of CFCs will be banned, recovery and recycling of refrigerant and the use of substitute refrigerants and retrofit systems will eventually be the only way of maintaining systems originally designed for

Important Note

No refrigerant other than R-12 should be used in an older passenger car air-conditioning system unless it is specifically recommended as a substitute for use in the system you are servicing by the original vehicle or air-conditioning system manufacturer. The installation of a substitute refrigerant will also require system modifications which must be done in conformance with the manufacturer's recommendations.

R-12. Becoming certified, and performing recovery and recycling work properly and according to federal and state requirements and industry standards, will also allow you to be in compliance with the law.

1.5 Legal Requirements

Any time your work involves automotive air-conditioning refrigerant you must meet the legal requirements of the EPA. These requirements are stated as follows:

Effective January 1, 1992, no person repairing or servicing motor vehicles for consideration may perform any service on a motor vehicle air conditioner involving the refrigerant for such air conditioner:

1.) without properly using equipment approved pursuant to ¤ 82.36 [SAE Standards J1989, J1990, and J1991] and

2.) unless such person has been properly trained and certified under ¤ 82.40 [an EPA approved training and certification program (see 40 CFR, Parts 82.40 and 82.42)][1].

From a practical viewpoint, these regulations require that service technicians operate equipment for extraction, recovery, and recycling refrigerant in accordance with the equipment manufacturer's instructions and the SAE standards that have been included, with minor changes, in the Code of Federal Regulations. (SAE J1989, J1990, J2209 as well as ARI Standard 700-93).

Federal certification and record-keeping requirements appear in Appendix B of this book.

1.6 Proper Procedures and the Right Equipment

The remainder of this book will acquaint you with the proper refrigerant extraction (also called "recovery" by some equipment manufacturers) and recycling techniques to provide "like new" air-conditioning performance without harming our environment.

It is important that you use only equipment designed specifically for these tasks. Furthermore, because different refrigerants have different characteristics, it is important that the equipment you use is compatible with the refrigerant with which you are working.

Before you start work, be certain you know:

1.) the type of refrigerant used in the system on which you will be working;

2.) that the recovery or recycling equipment is compatible with the refrigerant and meets appropriate federal, state, and SAE standards;

3.) that the equipment is free of all contaminants, including other refrigerants[2], and

4.) the correct service procedures, connection points, and equipment operating procedures.

---

[1] "Protection of Statospheric Ozone," Code of Federal Regulations, Title 40, Chapter 1, EPA Part 82.34, revised as of July 1, 1994.

[2] SAE strongly recommends that you use a dedicated piece of equipment for each refrigerant.

2. General Safety and Service Precautions

2.1 Safety

The refrigerants with which you will be working have potentially dangerous physical and chemical properties. All refrigerants are stored under relatively high pressure as a liquid, and all of them are chemicals which can be harmful or fatal if treated improperly. As such, they must be treated with respect. To do otherwise can expose you to physical injury, frostbite, blindness, possible poisoning and/or death by asphyxiation or cardiac arrest. In addition, some of the new refrigerants including R-134a have been found to be flammable under certain conditions. You should review the material safety data sheet (MSDS) provided by the refrigerant manufacturer for safe and proper handling information as well as instructions as to what to do if an emergency should arise. Read and understand the applicable MSDSs before you begin work on an air-conditioning system.

Likewise, your service equipment comes with a thorough set of operating instructions which should allow you to perform refrigeration system service work easily, efficiently, and safely. Read and understand the operating instructions for your service equipment before you start work.

The following safety warnings are generally recognized as minimum precautions that must be observed when servicing air-conditioning systems:

1.) Read, understand, and follow the instructions provided by the manufacturers of all the service and vehicle equipment with which you will be working.

2.) Wear safety goggles at all times when servicing an air-conditioning system, extraction or recycling equipment, or otherwise handling refrigerant. Liquid splashed in the eye can cause frostbite and/or irritation.

   Wear appropriate rubber gloves and other clothing whenever there is a potential for splashing liquid refrigerant on your skin. The refrigerant is a solvent for natural oils and will dry out your skin, causing irritation and cracking. Read and follow the information in the Material Safety Data Sheet provided by your refrigerant supplier regarding the proper handling of refrigerant.

3.) CAUTION: Refrigerant and lubricants can cause health problems.

   Avoid breathing AC refrigerant and lubricant vapor or mist. Exposure may irritate eyes, nose, and throat. To remove R-134a from the AC system, use service equipment certified to meet the requirements of SAE J2210 (R-134a recycling equipment). If accidental system discharge occurs, ventilate work area before resuming service. Additional health and safety information may be obtained from refrigerant and lubricant manufacturers.

   The oil used with R-134a refrigerant may irritate skin. Wear oil-proof gloves to protect yourself when handling these lubricants.

4.) CAUTION: Do not pressure test or leak test HFC-134a service equipment or vehicle air conditioning systems with compressed air. Some mixtures of air and HFC-134a have been shown to be combustible at elevated pressures. These mixtures, if ignited, may cause injury or property damage. Additional health and safety information may be obtained from refrigerant manufacturers.

5.) Never perform service operations other than routine maintenance on your extraction or recycling equipment without first consulting the manufacturers' authorized service personnel. Removal of fittings and filters can cause refrigerant under pressure to escape. Use the proper safety equipment, including safety goggles.

6.) Never service or maintain extraction or recycling equipment while it is plugged in unless proper service procedures direct you to do so.

7.) Always transfer refrigerant to cylinders or tanks specifically approved for refilling by the U.S. Department of Transportation. The designations "DOT 4BW" or "DOT 4BA" indicate such approval. Use no other containers.

8.) Never overfill a refrigerant container. There must be vapor space left in the cylinder in order to accommodate temperature-induced changes in pressure and liquid volume. SAE recommends filling tanks for shop use with liquid to no more than 60% of their gross weight rating.

9.) Ensure that containers are never heated to over 125 °F. Even a correctly filled container becomes an explosion hazard if its temperature exceeds 125 °F.

10.) Electrically operated equipment including extraction and recycling equipment may create sparks or arcs in internal switches or other systems. Because of the fire and explosion hazard that may be present, always use it in locations with forced ventilation having at least four air changes per hour.

11.) Extension cords are a known cause of fires and equipment malfunction. Their use is not recommended. In circumstances where their use is unavoidable, the shortest cord with 14 gauge or larger conductors must be used. If your service equipment requires a ground circuit (third prong), make sure that the extension cord is so equipped and that the ground circuit is intact. Avoid cords that are worn, frayed, or otherwise damaged.

12.) Perform work only in well-ventilated areas. Some refrigerants can accumulate in low areas such as service pits. Breathing concentrated refrigerant vapors could result in asphyxiation or other health hazards, including cardiac arrest.

2.2 Cleanliness

Many failures in all types of systems can be traced to dirt. The cleaner your work, the longer your customers' systems will last, and the less need there will be for maintenance operations that will potentially release refrigerant into the atmosphere.

Dirt, even microscopic particles, in hose and pipe connections can create enough clearance for the refrigerant to escape. Research has shown that some flexible hoses in used but otherwise "perfect" R-12 systems may lose up to 0.1 kg (0.2 lb) or more of refrigerant per year.[3] Imagine how much will leak through a hose fitting held apart a few hundredths of a thousandth of an inch by a piece of dirt!

---

[3] Lemmons and Bradow, "Refrigerant R-12 Leakage in Automobile Air Conditioner Systems," SAE Paper No. 810506, presented at the International Congress and Exposition, Detroit, Michigan, February 23-27, 1981.

2.3 Check for Leaks First

2.3.1 Background

In addition to providing your customer with a reliable, properly functioning air-conditioning system, a major objective of air-conditioning service is to minimize the amount of refrigerant that escapes into the atmosphere. You can go a long way toward achieving both of these objectives by identifying any major leaks in the system before it is recharged with more refrigerant. (The exception to this might be in the case where so much refrigerant has leaked out that there is insufficient pressure left to identify all but the largest leaks. In this case, partially recharging the system to 50 psi with the recommended refrigerant should be sufficient for checking leaks.)

"Topping off" a leaky air-conditioning system perpetuates the escape of refrigerant to the atmosphere. Therefore, this procedure is not an accepted method of returning a poorly performing system to service. The proper service procedure is to locate and then correct the leak before putting any refrigerant into a system.

Important Notes

- Any refrigerant introduced into the system for the purpose of finding leaks must also be recovered without releasing it into the atmosphere.

- Always use the same type of refrigerant for checking for leaks as was either originally installed into the AC system by the manufacturer, or was retrofitted.

- Never use compressed or shop air to detect system leaks. The introduction of air into the system may create a fire or explosion hazard, may overload the desiccant with moisture, and could contaminate the system with dirt and oil as well.

All automotive air-conditioning systems leak to some extent.[3] When servicing them, it is important that leakage be minimized. Much of the "normal" leakage comes from the slow seepage of refrigerant through the flexible hoses. Other common sources of leaks are at the joints between the flexible hose and metal tubing or at threaded hose connections. These are usually much larger leaks than the natural seepage through the walls of the hose and are almost always repairable.

In order to minimize damage to the environment, you should repair leaks that are 1/2 ounce per year or more. Detection of such leaks is difficult, and requires both the proper equipment and the proper technique. Both are covered by SAE standards discussed later in this chapter.

Research by the EPA has found that:

> "Leak detection can be difficult, but existing halogen leak detection systems are adequate for the major task of finding and repairing gross leaks causing customer complaints. Apparently, dye stains are not very satisfactory for finding small leaks."[3]

Portable halogen leak detectors were found by EPA researchers to detect some leaks that die-laced refrigerant did not detect. Newer electronic leak checkers may offer even better leak detection capabilities. However, no method can be relied on to find all leaks.

Even so, electronic leak detectors may not detect leaks of all refrigerants. For example, older units designed to detect R-12 may not detect R-134a. Be sure that the leak detector you use is state-of-the-art and that it is designed to detect leaks of the refrigerant that is in the system you are servicing. It should also meet SAE Standard J1627 and be labeled as such.

Under no circumstances should you attempt to detect a leak with a match or a flame-type leak detector. It was never a very good idea to have an open flame under the hood of a car. With the increasing prices and future shortages of R-12, there is a distinct possibility that the system you are servicing may have been filled or topped-off with a flammable material such as propane. If so, a flame-type detector or match could ignite the flammable refrigerant and cause a fire, personal injury, severe damage to the vehicle, or other catastrophic results.

If you are unsure of the type of refrigerant in the system you are servicing, you can use one of the refrigerant contaminant detectors to help you identify a system that has been retrofitted with a new refrigerant, possible contaminants, or hazardous refrigerants. Use a refrigerant contaminant detector approved by the manufacturer of the vehicle on which you are working. At some future time, an applicable SAE Standard may be developed. When such a standard is developed, you should use equipment meeting that standard.

Just because a leak can't be detected doesn't mean it isn't there. Service professionals must be extremely diligent in their work to detect all leaks possible. Diligence is also necessary to ensure that the workmanship used in system repair and assembly is of the highest quality to avoid small, undetectable leaks.

The last thing you should do before closing the hood is to check the system for leaks. One last leak check may uncover that fitting that isn't quite tight or that was assembled with just a little bit of dirt. Catching the leak just after service will save both you and your customer an inconvenient and expensive return visit ("come-back") later.

2.3.2 Leak Detection Equipment

Leak detection must meet SAE Standard J1627. Look for a label that states: "Design Certified by (Certifying Agent such as Underwriters Laboratories or equivalent) to meet SAE J1627 for (Refrigerant type or types inserted here)."

Your responsibility goes beyond just selecting the proper piece of equipment. You must follow the manufacturer's instructions for maintenance and calibration. If the leak detector gives you any indication that it is out of calibration, you should repair it immediately. Buy, borrow, or rent a properly functioning leak detector to use while yours is being repaired and recalibrated. Do not use a leak detector that is out of calibration or is malfunctioning. To do so could result in your doing unnecessary repairs or not detecting a leak that will cause a come-back.

2.3.3 Proper Use of Leak Detection Equipment (see SAE Standard J1628):

1.) Be sure there is adequate pressure in the system to detect a leak. Hook up your manifold gauge set and be sure that there is at least 50 psi (340 kPa) pressure in the system. If the system needs to be charged, be sure to charge it with the same refrigerant recommended by the vehicle manufacturer or that in accordance with any retrofit label. (**Caution:** Leak testing should not be done below 59 °F [15 °C] because even a properly charged system may not have at least 50 psi [340 kPa] pressure.)

2.) Use a fan to ventilate the engine compartment before you test for leaks. In addition to refrigerants, leak detectors can also sense some non-refrigerant chemicals such as antifreeze, brake cleaners, diesel fuel, and other common automotive chemicals such as solvents. Ensuring that there is fresh air under the hood will minimize the influence of these chemicals on your leak detector. Turn off the fan when you do the leak test, and, of course, be sure the engine is not running.

3.) Test for leaks by tracing along all system components with the leak detector probe. Hold the probe tip 1/4 inch (5 mm) or closer to the system components being checked. Move it along at a speed of about 1 to 2 inches per second. The slower you go, the more likely you are to find a leak.

Pay special attention to those areas that show lubricant leakage, damage, corrosion, or any other visible signs of a potential leak. Be sure to check all fittings, hose-to-line couplings, refrigerant controls, service ports (with caps in place), brazed or welded joints, areas around brackets or hold-down points, and the compressor shaft seal.

The evaporator core may be tested immediately after running the blower on "high" for at least 15 seconds. After you shut the blower off, wait for the "accumulation time" specified in the instructions for your leak detector. Then test the evaporator case area by putting your leak detector's probe into the case, near the evaporator, through the blower resistor block, the condensate drain hole (if there is no water present), or into the closest opening in the ducting leading from the evaporator. This procedure ensures that there is enough time for a leak in the evaporator to show up without falsely triggering your detector from refrigerant gas that has entered into the evaporator case from other sources.

As you trace the system, keep the probe tip clean. If you bump a greasy or dirty spot, be sure to clean the tip as recommended by the detector manufacturer. Do not use a solvent cleaner, as the detector may confuse the solvent with a refrigerant leak.

4.) Verify all detected leaks at least once by blowing shop air at the suspected leak and rechecking for the leak with your detector. This procedure may also help you pinpoint the exact location of a leak if you find refrigerant present over a large area.

5.) If a leak is found, continue to check the remainder of the system. Always be sure that you have found all of the leaks.

2.4 Filling

Refilling an air-conditioning system must be done by the weight method. Visual methods of refilling R-134a systems will result in improper system charging. For example, the lubricants used with R-134a tend to layer onto the walls of the refrigeration system. This layering obscures the view through the sight glass. Also, properly charged R-134a systems may show bubbles in the sight glass while others may not. For these reasons, the old practice of "topping off" a partially discharged air-conditioning system using the sight glass is still not recommended.

3. Refrigerant and System Properties

3.1 Cooling Characteristics

Each refrigerant has certain physical properties which make it ideal for some applications. Because each type of refrigeration system is designed for a specific purpose, a particular refrigerant has been selected for that system. Traditionally, the refrigerant of choice for mobile air-conditioning systems has been R-12. The ozone-safe alternative, R-134a, has also been developed to satisfy the requirements of mobile air-conditioning systems.

No two refrigerants are alike. Each refrigerant has its own set of physical properties. No refrigeration system will perform equally well or for as long if its original refrigerant is replaced with a type not specifically approved for that application.

In one test, for example, R-12 was replaced with R-134a in a typical system. Compressor discharge pressures were about 175 kPa (25 psi) higher while the discharge temperature was about 8 °C (14 °F) colder.[4] Other tests[5] indicate that system performance is particularly reduced under slow-speed city driving conditions, precisely when AC is most often needed. In any case, operation outside the system design limits could seriously impair system performance or result in an overload and failure. In either case, the customer would not be pleased.

3.2 Lubricants

The lubricant and the refrigerant are developed as a system. Researchers seeking environmentally friendly replacements for CFCs have found that it is necessary to develop totally new lubricant packages if compressor life with HFCs or HCFCs is to be equal to that of CFCs. R-134a, for example, causes the mineral oil used with the R-12 to become chemically unstable. Therefore, R-134a will likely use a lubricant made from polyalkylene glycols (PAG), although polyolester or fluorochemicals are also being considered. None of these lubricants is compatible with the mineral oil used with R-12.

Likewise, the hoses, bearing shaft seals, and O-rings used in the system are not compatible with all lubricants. Hardening, swelling, or cracking of these rubber parts when used with incompatible lubricants will also lead to early failure of the system.

Lubricant/rubber compatibility will be particularly critical with the new refrigerants. The lubricants for R-134a and some of the HCFCs are far more aggressive to rubber parts than the old mineral oils. When servicing air-conditioning systems, be certain that the rubber parts you are installing are approved for use with the lubricants in the system. The use of OEM or aftermarket parts from reputable automotive suppliers is your best approach.

Even though all R-134a systems may use PAG-based lubricants, the lubricant additive package used by each vehicle or AC system manufacturer may be different. While the base-stock of PAG lubricant may be the same,

---

[4] "Refrigerant Changes for A/C Systems," *Automotive Engineering*, Vol. 99, No. 2, February, 1991, pp. 25-29.
[5] Bateman, "Performance Comparison of HFC 134a and CFC-12 in an Automotive Air Conditioning System," SAE Paper No. 890305, presented at the International Congress and Exposition, Detroit, Michigan, February 27 - March 3, 1989.

the additive packages are not always compatible. Therefore, unlike older mineral-based systems where most any AC mineral oil would suffice, only the PAG lubricants specifically recommended by the vehicle or AC system manufacturer should be used. This will be true for the retrofit systems as well.

In summary, it is important that you use only the correct lubricant for the system you are servicing. Use only the lubricant recommended by the system manufacturer. On newer systems, the lubricant will be specified on an identification tag mounted in the engine compartment, on a body structure or air-conditioning system component.

3.3 Contaminants

3.3.1 "Naturally Occurring" Contaminants

No mobile air-conditioning system can operate for long without naturally picking up some contaminants in the refrigerant. The flexible hoses, for example, allow moisture to migrate into the refrigerant from the outside atmosphere. In laboratory tests, this moisture has reacted with CFC and HCFC refrigerants to form hydrochloric acid. Moisture and noncondensable gases (air) are the most common contaminants found in mobile air-conditioning systems. Acids are not normally present in mobile air conditioning systems. However, they are most often found contaminating refrigerants that have been extracted from non-mobile air conditioning systems.

Tests by Du Pont [6] have shown that various contaminants will encourage the formation of a copper plating on the surfaces of steel AC system parts. This happens when R-134a and PAG lubricants are contaminated with CFC-11 or a mixture of mineral oil and R-12 and used in a system with some copper or brass parts. The copper is actually transferred from the original part to a steel part. Significant plating can lead to major compressor failures.

Lubricant and even refrigerant that remains in service equipment can be a contaminant. The lubricant may have absorbed some refrigerant, moisture, and air that has migrated into the air-conditioning system. Some of the lubricant is captured by and carried along with the refrigerant. When you recover a refrigerant, a certain amount of lubricant will be captured by the extraction or recycling equipment as well. This lubricant will be drained into a catch bottle or reservoir for measurement and proper final disposal.

Lubricant that has come out of an air-conditioning system should never be reused. Reusing this oil may result in contamination of the air-conditioning system with the refrigerant, moisture, and air that has been temporarily absorbed into the oil. Instead, the AC system should be refilled with the same amount of fresh oil that was removed in the service operation. The used oils must be safely disposed of in a manner which complies with federal, state, and local disposal requirements.

To avoid contamination between systems using dissimilar refrigerants, the SAE recommends that extraction and recycling equipment be dedicated to a single type of refrigerant UNLESS the equipment has been certified as meeting SAE Standard J1770 as being suitable for use with either R-12 or R-134a [7]. This is the best way to ensure that there is no cross-contamination of lubricants and other impurities from systems using different refrigerants. Proper and thorough flushing of all contaminants from service equipment so that it can be used with a different refrigerant requires a second piece of extraction or recycling machine to clean the first one. Furthermore, the technician's time devoted to flushing out the equipment could be better spent servicing a car.

---

[6] "Factors Affecting the Copper Plating Phenomena with HFC-134a/Polyalkylene Glycol Refrigerant Fluids," Du Pont Chemicals publication ARTD-32.

[7] As of this writing, SAE Standard J1770 is still under development. No equipment is expected to be certified to this standard until very late 1995 or 1996 at the earliest.

It is far more efficient for the service garage to dedicate each machine to a particular refrigerant than to use one machine to clean the other.

3.3.2 Intentionally Introduced Contaminants

With the reduction and eventual elimination of new sources of R-12, mobile AC systems using this refrigerant have been found to be contaminated with substances introduced by do-it-yourselfers or other service garages in attempt to "top-up" an R-12 system. These intentionally introduced contaminants can include propane, R-134a, or refrigerant blends such as R401c or FRGC. These contaminants may not only reduce the effectiveness of your customers' AC systems, but some, like propane, can create a fire or explosion hazard. Others can potentially damage your refrigerant recycling equipment, and all will contaminate the refrigerant already contained in your extraction or recycling equipment, rendering that material worthless. R-12 or R-134a that has been contaminated by another refrigerant cannot be purified by your in-shop recycling equipment.

3.3.3 Coping With Contaminants

To prevent contamination of the refrigerant in your extraction or recycling equipment, it is a good idea to check the refrigerant for type and possible contamination before you recover the refrigerant from any vehicle you service. As of this writing, the SAE has no recommended service procedure to deal with this situation, but they are developing a standard (SAE J1771) for equipment that will identify the type of refrigerant and/or contaminants in the air-conditioning system. Until SAE-certified equipment is available, you should use a device that has been approved for this purpose by the manufacturer of the vehicle on which you are working. Be sure to follow the equipment manufacturer's instructions carefully.

Refrigerant contaminated with other refrigerants or propane should be extracted using a separate piece of extraction equipment specially designed and dedicated for that purpose. Such equipment may be air-operated to minimize the risk of fire or explosion when handling refrigerant that may contain flammable gas such as propane. If you do not have such a piece of extraction equipment, you should send the vehicle to a shop that can safely handle the contaminated refrigerant.

Refrigerants contaminated with another refrigerant or propane must be sent out to a Certified Refrigerant Reclaimer who can specially treat this potentially hazardous refrigerant. Be sure to use a separate, DOT-approved container to store and transport the contaminated refrigerant. Do NOT vent it.

3.4 Why Prevent Mixing of Different Types of Refrigerants in Service Equipment?

Refrigerants must not be mixed. For this reason, compressor service fittings are supposed to be different for refrigerants R-12 and R-134a. SAE J2197 establishes unique service hose fittings for refrigeration systems using R-134a. Systems using R-134a have quick couple service connections while R-12 systems use screw threads. The intent of this is to prevent the use of the same tools for different refrigerants, thereby avoiding mixing of refrigerants in the service equipment.

Incompatible lubricants and other contaminants can be left behind on air-conditioning service manifolds, gages, hoses, and fittings. Even small amounts of refrigerant and lubricant left behind can be harmful to the performance and durability of a system designed to use another refrigerant.

At the least, significant amounts of the incorrect refrigerant will cause poor cooling performance, resulting in an unhappy customer and a "come-back." At the other extreme, the thermodynamic and chemical characteristics of some refrigerants will result in excessive pressure and poor lubrication, leading to possible failure of the compressor, desiccant, and other system components. Mixtures of R-12 and R-134a can result in up to 25% overpressure.

In addition, refrigerants carry with them varying amounts of contaminants. Chief among these are air, moisture, and the lubricating oil used in the compressor. As previously discussed, some of these lubricants are incompatible with each other as well as with some refrigerants. Furthermore, some of the materials used for hoses and seals may be attacked and ruined if they come into contact with the incorrect lubricant.

Therefore, care must be taken to dedicate the use of service equipment to a particular refrigerant, and to avoid contamination of each piece of equipment with the wrong refrigerant. Ultimate system failure and an expensive repair bill may result if refrigerants are mixed in a single set of service equipment. For these reasons, the SAE recommends that separate and dedicated equipment be used to service R-12 and R-134a systems until equipment capable of dealing with both refrigerants (and avoiding contamination of one with the other) has been developed to meet pending SAE Standard J1770.

4. Equipment for the Extraction-only of Refrigerant and Equipment for the Recycling of Refrigerant

4.1 What's the Difference?

Both "extraction" and "recycling" equipment are in use and available to automotive service technicians. Both types of equipment will remove the refrigerant from a vehicle's air-conditioning system. However, extraction equipment only pulls the refrigerant from the air-conditioning system and stores it in an approved container. Extraction equipment does not clean the refrigerant. Its only use is to recover the refrigerant from an air-conditioning system prior to disassembling and servicing it.

It is important that recovered refrigerant is recycled or reclaimed before it is put back into an air-conditioning system. During service operations involving a partial recharge or while the AC system is in use, refrigerant can pick up moisture, lubricants, microscopic metal chips, and other potential contaminants. In many cases, these contaminants contributed to or are the primary cause of the refrigeration system failure. To put used but uncleaned refrigerant back into an air-conditioning system may well result in poor system performance, a dissatisfied customer, and a "come-back." Reuse of refrigerant that has not been recycled or reclaimed may also void vehicle manufacturers' warranties.

There is a danger that equipment that removes refrigerant from a mobile air-conditioning system (usually called "recovery" equipment) may allow the service technician to put the used refrigerant back into the system without first cleaning it to minimum performance standards. There is also the danger that such equipment may be used to pull refrigerant from non-mobile air-conditioning systems. Non-mobile air-conditioning systems use refrigerants and contain contaminants that are different from those in mobile air-conditioning systems. Recovery equipment may therefore allow the mixing of different types of refrigerants or introduce contaminants that may not be removable by recycling equipment available in the service shop.

Extraction equipment meeting SAE J2209 has unique fittings that make impossible the inadvertent recharging of mobile air-conditioning systems with uncleaned refrigerant. While both recovery and extraction equipment will pull refrigerant from mobile air-conditioning systems, only extraction equipment meeting SAE J2209 should be used for this purpose. Machines meeting SAE J2209 allow the used refrigerant to be stored in approved containers until the refrigerant can be taken to a recycling center where it can be reclaimed to levels of purity established for refrigerant by the Air-conditioning and Refrigeration Institute (ARI standard 700-93 or newer).

If you want to remove, clean, and reuse the same refrigerant at your shop, you must use a machine that both extracts and recycles refrigerant from mobile air-conditioning systems. Such equipment is usually called "recycling equipment." Recycling equipment meeting SAE standards (SAE J1990 and J2210) is capable of removing the contaminants normally found in mobile air-conditioning systems so that the extracted refrigerant is safe to use once again. Alternatively, you can recover the refrigerant with extraction equipment and then recycle it by transferring it to your recycling equipment. However, the EPA regulations require that both the extraction equipment and the recycling equipment be owned by the same service establishment to minimize the possibility of contamination. Refrigerant that has been properly cleaned with recycling equipment can be charged back into an air-conditioning system, meets SAE standards of purity (SAE J1991 for R-12 and J2099 for R-134a), and will provide "like new" performance.

It is important to note that recycling equipment meeting SAE standards J1990 and J2210 is designed to extract and treat refrigerants that have been in mobile air-conditioning systems only. R-12 and R-134a refrigerants may also be used in non-mobile air-conditioning or refrigeration systems. Non-mobile systems may introduce contaminants to the refrigerant that equipment meeting SAE J1990 and J2210 cannot remove. For example, non-mobile air-conditioning systems are known to generate acids that are not expected to be found in mobile systems. Equipment conforming to SAE J1990 and J2210 is not intended to deal with these acids.

4.2 Using Extraction Equipment

Extraction equipment is relatively small and easily portable. It is best used in situations where a shop must service vehicles such as agricultural or off-highway equipment that cannot easily be brought into the shop. It is also convenient for shops that must deal with a variety of different refrigerant types and exchange recovered refrigerant for reclaimed refrigerant at some central location.

It is most important that extraction equipment is used only for those refrigerants for which it is designed. The lubricants, hoses, and seals in this equipment have been designed to work with only a limited range of refrigerants. Use with incompatible refrigerants could result in expensive damage to the machine.

To help avoid a mix-up of service equipment and refrigerants, equipment hoses designed for use with each refrigerant will be easier to identify. New service hose compatible with R-12 will carry the designation "SAE J2196." Service hose used with R-134a must have a black stripe along its length and carry the designation "SAE J2196/R-134a." (See Figure 2.)

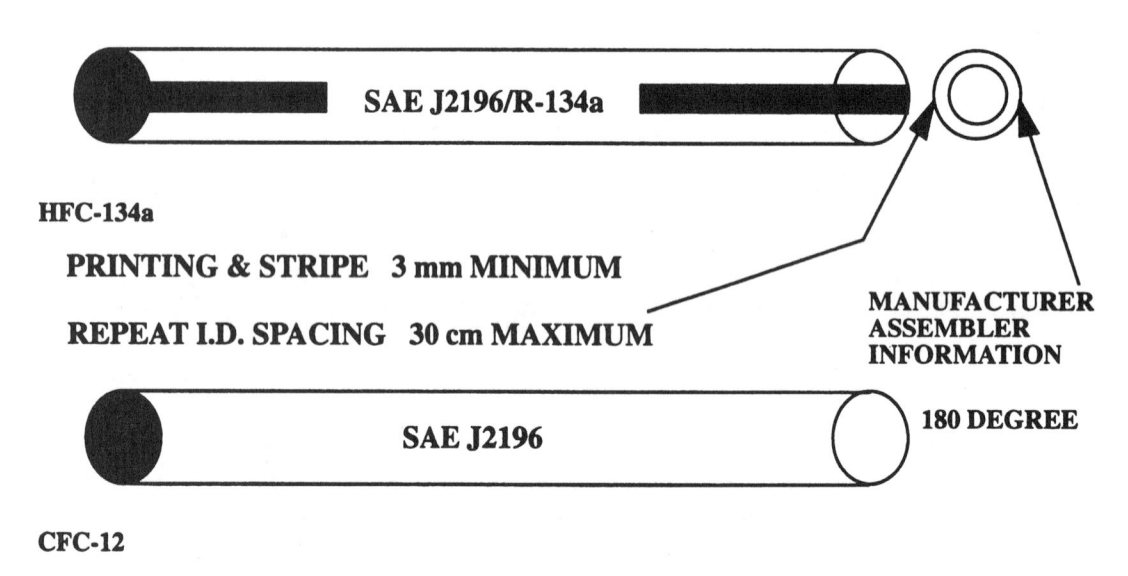

Figure 2—J2196 Service Hose

It is important to note that when substitute refrigerants and retrofit kits are developed for servicing R-12-based systems, current service equipment may not be compatible with these new refrigerants. A separate set of service equipment will be required for each refrigerant used. To date, no SAE standards exist for refrigerants or service equipment other than those for R-12 and R-134a.

If you use extraction equipment and send your recovered refrigerant "outside" to a reclamation facility, reclaimed refrigerant you purchase should be certified to meet the Air-conditioning and Refrigeration Institute standards of purity (ARI Standard 700-93 or newer for R-12). This will ensure that the refrigerant you are using not only meets the purity requirements of SAE J1991 (for R-12) or J2099 (for R-134a), but also that it does not contain incompatible lubricants or other contaminants from non-automotive air-conditioning systems.

Because extraction equipment cannot recycle refrigerant, it is not certified as meeting SAE J1990 (for R-12) or J2210 (for R-134a). Extraction equipment that meets SAE J2209 avoids the inadvertent reuse of unreclaimed R-12.

4.3 Using Recycling Equipment

Recycling equipment is defined as equipment that both extracts and removes common contaminants from refrigerants. Recycling equipment designed and certified to meet SAE standards can make refrigerant recovered from mobile air-conditioning systems suitable for reuse in automotive AC systems. Like extraction equipment, SAE recommends that you dedicate each piece of recycling equipment to a single refrigerant.

Note that only equipment capable of recovering and cleaning R-12 to meet SAE J1991 purity levels can be certified as meeting SAE J1990. Only equipment capable of recovering and cleaning R-134a to meet SAE J2099 purity levels can be certified as meeting SAE Standard J2210.

Underwriters Laboratories and other equivalent organizations can certify recycling equipment. Equipment capable of purifying CFC-12 (R-12) to SAE J1991 levels of purity will carry a label which contains the phrase "Design certified by Underwriters Laboratories, Inc. (or equivalent), for compliance with SAE J1991 (1989)."[8] Recycling equipment capable of purifying HFC-134a (R-134a) to SAE J2099 purity levels will carry a label which contains the phrase "Design certified by Underwriters Laboratories, Inc. (or equivalent) for compliance with SAE J2099 (1992)." Note that the Underwriters Laboratories label which certifies that the machine is free of reasonable shock or other safety hazards to the user is **NOT** an indication of compliance with SAE standards. The certification label must specifically state that the machine is "Design certified" to the applicable SAE standard[9].

4.4 Recycling versus Reclaiming

Recycled refrigerant is refrigerant that has been recovered from a mobile air-conditioning system and which is cleaned to meet SAE J1991 or J2099 by the same shop that recovered it. The equipment designed to recycle refrigerant in the shop environment is intended to remove only those types of contaminants that are picked up during the operation of mobile air-conditioning equipment.

Reclaimed refrigerant has been recovered from a variety of different shops and possibly even different types of air-conditioning systems, and has then been reprocessed to the same standards of purity as virgin refrigerant. Reclamation to such standards of purity requires equipment that is normally not affordable by the average automotive service shop. Hence, reclamation of refrigerant is usually done by independent companies established for that purpose.

For all intents and purposes, both properly recycled and properly reclaimed refrigerant will provide adequate service in mobile air-conditioning systems.

---

[8] or the most recent year standard to which that machine complies
[9] As of May, 1995, both Underwriters Laboratories and ETL Testing Laboratories are approved, independent testing organizations certifying equipment to SAE standards.

5. Service Procedure for the Containment of Automotive Air-Conditioning Refrigerants

5.1 Purpose

This section is intended as a guide to servicing mobile air-conditioning systems in a way that minimizes the potential for losing refrigerant to the atmosphere. Following the procedures in this section will help you ensure compliance with SAE J1989 for R-12 systems and J2211 for R-134a systems.

Safety Notice for R-134a (HFC-134a) Refrigerants

Fire or explosion hazard exists with R-134a (HFC-134a) under certain conditions. R-134a has been shown to be nonflammable at ambient temperature and atmospheric pressure. However, tests under controlled conditions have indicated that, at pressures above atmospheric and with air concentrations greater than 60% by volume, R-134a can form combustible mixtures. While it is recognized that an ignition source is also required for combustion to occur, the presence of combustible mixtures is a potentially dangerous situation and should be avoided.

CAUTION: R-134a service equipment or vehicle air-conditioning systems should not be pressure tested or leak tested with compressed air. Some mixtures of air/R-134a have been shown to be combustible at elevated pressures. These mixtures are potentially dangerous and may result in fire or explosion causing injury or property damage. Additional health and safety information may be obtained from refrigerant and lubricant manufacturers.

5.2 Refrigerant Recovery Procedure

1.) Ensure that all equipment hose lines are fitted with shut-off valves within 12 inches (30 cm) of their ends. This will ensure that only minimal quantities of refrigerant escape to the atmosphere when the system is disconnected from the refrigeration system, and that only small amounts of moisture and other contaminants can enter the system.

2.) Be sure that all equipment including the connecting hose lines and manifold are compatible with the refrigerant in the system on which you are going to work, and that your equipment has been previously used only with the refrigerant you are about to service.

Important Note

Shut-off valves should be closed at all times unless they are connected to a vehicle's air conditioning system, a refrigerant storage container, or another piece of service apparatus containing the same refrigerant. This prevents refrigerant from escaping into the atmosphere, damaging the environment, and costing you money.

3.) Be certain that all shut-off valves are shut tight before connecting them to the refrigeration system.

4.) Taking the advice of Chapter 2 - General Safety and Service Precautions, and observing all other safety practices, connect the extraction equipment meeting SAE J2209 for R-12, or the recovery or the recycling equipment meeting SAE J1990 for R-12 systems, or J2210 for R-134a systems to the air-conditioning system in accordance with the instructions supplied by the equipment and vehicle manufacturers. Since the service fittings used on R-134a systems are similar to those used on some fuel injection systems, double-check to make sure that you are connecting your equipment to the air-conditioning system and not the fuel system.

5.) Start the recovery process by turning on the machine and extracting the refrigerant from the vehicle refrigeration system in accordance with the equipment manufacturer's instructions.

6.) Continue to extract refrigerant until the refrigeration system has been brought under a vacuum and there is no refrigerant remaining in the vehicle system. Gentle warming of the driers and/or accumulators with a hair dryer or similar, flameless heat source may speed the extraction process by vaporizing any refrigerant mixed with lube oil or trapped by water that may have accumulated in these parts. Natural vaporization of the refrigerant may cause frosting on the outside of these or other components. Do not warm them with your hand as frostbite or freezing of your skin to the metal parts may occur.

7.) Verify that there is no refrigerant remaining in the system by:

   a.) Shutting off the extraction unit and observing the system pressure level.

   b.) Waiting five minutes and observing the system pressure again. If system pressure has not risen above atmospheric pressure ("0" gauge pressure), all the refrigerant has been removed and you may proceed with step 8.

   If, after five minutes, the system pressure reading has risen above atmospheric pressure ("0" gauge pressure), the extraction/recovery process must be repeated until the pressure reading remains at or below atmospheric for at least two minutes with the extraction equipment shut off before proceeding to step 8.

8.) Close the shut-off valves in the service lines.

9.) Remove the service lines from the vehicle system. If the recovery equipment has automatic closing shut-off valves, verify that they are operating properly and do not leak.

10.) Determine the amount of lubricant removed from the AC system during the refrigerant extraction process. Replenish the AC system with an equal volume of the new, recommended lubricant. (Vehicles produced after 1991 should have a label on the compressor specifying the recommended lubricant.)

   Dispose of the used lubricant in accordance with applicable federal, state, and local requirements. At this point, you are ready to undertake service and repair procedures.

5.3 Flushing

Some service or repair operations recommend flushing the AC system to remove dirt or other debris. It has been common practice to use another CFC, usually R-11, for this purpose. The Clean Air Act prohibits the use of any CFC for such a purpose **where the CFC may be released to the atmosphere**. Methylchloroform (1,1,1 trichloroethane), a popular flushing agent, is also prohibited by the Montreal Protocol.

Flushing should never be done with shop or other compressed air. Certain mixtures of air and R-134a are combustible. The use of air to flush R-134a systems could result in combustion. Shop air also contains moisture which could use up the system desiccant, causing an early come-back and additional costs for the customer. Never use CFC-11, R-11, CFC-12, R-12, CFC-113, R-113, or any other substance to flush an R-134a (HFC-134a) system. To do so may result in breakdown of the lubricant or system corrosion.

Use of other flushing solvents may cause other problems. If a vacuum pump does not remove the solvent, it could affect the chemical stability of the refrigerant and lubricant.

The practice of open vent flushing will often not remove failed compressor material from condenser units. Some AC system manufacturers recommend that flushing not be performed after a mechanical failure. The use of an in-line filter is considered the more effective method of controlling debris resulting from component failures.

If you think it necessary to flush the system because, for example, of a catastrophic compressor failure, you must power closed-circuit flush the various sections of the system with refrigerant designed for use in that system. Be sure to recover all of the refrigerant used for flushing. It is illegal to vent it. You may still elect to add a system filter, however, because flushing may not remove all the debris.

5.4 Recharge/Refilling

Remember to recharge the system only with the proper virgin refrigerant or recycled refrigerant purified to meet SAE purity standards (J1991 for R-12 or J2099 for R-134a) or reclaimed R-12 refrigerant meeting ARI standard 700-93 or newer. Recharge in accordance with the vehicle or system manufacturer's instructions using an approved refrigerant. Use the weight method to determine the proper amount of refrigerant.

5.5 Use of a Manifold Gauge Set

When using a manifold gauge set to diagnose, recharge, or service a mobile air-conditioning system:

1.) Ensure that all equipment hose lines are fitted with shut-off valves within 12 inches (30 cm) of their ends and that the valves are closed. This will ensure that only minimal quantities of refrigerant escape to the atmosphere when the system is disconnected from the refrigeration system, and that only small amounts of moisture and other contaminants can enter the system.

2.) Be sure that all equipment including the connecting hose lines and manifold are compatible with the refrigerant in the AC system, free of all contaminants, and used only for the same type of refrigerant in the AC system.

3.) Be certain that all shut-off valves are shut tight before connecting them to the refrigeration system or charging source.

4.) Taking the advice of the General Safety and Service Precautions (Chapter 2), and observing all other safety practices, connect the manifold gauge set to the air-conditioning system in accordance with the instructions supplied by the equipment and vehicle manufacturers. Be sure you are connecting to the AC system and not similar-looking fuel injection system fittings.

5.) Perform your desired diagnosis and service operation.

6.) Close the shut-off valves on the service hoses.

7.) Disconnect the hoses from the system in accordance with equipment and vehicle manufacturers' instructions.

> ### Important Note
>
> When the manifold gauge set is disconnected from the air-conditioning system and you want to empty it of refrigerant, or when the center hose is to be moved to another device which cannot accept refrigerant pressure, the hoses should first be attached to recovery equipment or recycling equipment meeting SAE J1990 (for R-12) or J2210 (for R-134a) to remove the refrigerant, lubricant, and contaminants from the hoses.

5.6 Checking Refrigerant for Excess Air

At times you may question whether a container of refrigerant has been recycled. One check which can be done in the shop is to determine if there is excess air mixed in with the refrigerant. This check is a simple comparison of the container pressure with a theoretical pressure at a known temperature. If the pressure is equal to or less than a theoretical value established for R-12 or R-134a of usable purity, the contents of the container do not contain excess air.

Note that the use of refrigerant with excess air will result in higher system operating pressures and may cause damage to the AC system.

This check can be done in the following manner:

1.) Store the container for at least 12 hours at a known temperature of 65 °F (18.3 °C) or higher. The container must not be in direct sunlight or under the influence of any other direct source of heat.

    Carry out all of the next steps in the same area in which the container has been stored, as it is very important that the temperature of the container is stable.

2.) Attach an appropriate pressure gauge to the container. This pressure gauge should read in increments of 1 psi (6.9 kPa).

3.) Use a calibrated thermometer to measure the air temperature within 4 inches (10 cm) of the container surface.

4.) Compare the pressure in the container with the pressure shown for the temperature of the tank in Tables 1 or 2 of SAE J1989 for R-12 or J2211 for R-134a (see Appendix A). If the pressure in the container is equal to or less than the pressure in the tables, the refrigerant in the container meets the requirements for excess air. For example, if the temperature of an R-12 container (the same as the temperature of the requirements for room in which it has been stored for the last 12 hours or more) is 70 °F (21 °C) and the pressure you measure is 80 psi (5.6 kg/cm^2) or less, the R-12 in the container meets the requirements for excess air.

    If the pressure is greater than shown in the table, you may still be able to use it by proceeding to step 5.

5.) If the pressure exceeds that of the tables in SAE J1989 or J2211 (see the Appendix), connect the tank to recovery or recycling equipment in such a way as to allow you to continue to monitor tank pressure.

6.) Bleed a small amount of vapor from the tank into the recovery or recycling equipment until the tank pressure is below that shown in the appropriate table for the temperature at which the tank was stored. Then close the shut-off valves in the recovery/recycling equipment service hose.

Note that this process may cause the temperature of the tank to drop.

7.) Allow the tank temperature to restabilize at the temperature of the storage room by shaking it and allowing it to sit in the same spot for up to another 12 hours.

8.) After making certain that container temperature has again stabilized to room temperature, repeat step 4 above. If the pressure exceeds that in the appropriate tables for the storage temperature you measured, the refrigerant in the tank has too much excess air to be used and must be recycled or reclaimed.

If the refrigerant being checked has been contaminated with another refrigerant (e.g., R-12 and R-134a), the tank pressure may indicate it contains air. If the tank is vented and the pressures still indicate a high reading, the refrigerant may be contaminated and should be sent to a reclaim facility.

5.7 Containers for the Storage of Recycled Refrigerant

Recycled refrigerant must be stored only in DOT CFR Title 49 or UL (Underwriters Laboratories) containers approved for such use. The container must be specifically marked for the refrigerant type you are storing. The use of unmarked containers must be avoided as it can lead to mixing of refrigerants and consequent AC system failure.

Disposable refrigerant containers should not be used for the storage or recovery of used or recycled refrigerant. Disposable containers are the type of container in which virgin refrigerant is often sold.

Any container of recycled refrigerant that has been stored or transferred must be checked prior to its use in accordance with the temperature/pressure check described in Section 5.6, Checking Refrigerant for Excess Air. (See also Section 5 of SAE J1989 or J2211 in Appendix A.)

New storage tanks must be evacuated to at least 25 inches (635 mm) of mercury prior to use. Otherwise, excess air may be introduced to the refrigerant.

5.8 Transfer of Refrigerant

To transfer refrigerant in portable containers you must make sure that:

1.) The container meets DOT CFR Title 49 requirements and is UL-approved for such use.

2.) The container is free of contaminants and air. To ensure that the container is sufficiently free of air and contaminants, pull a vacuum of at least 25 inches of mercury (-13.26 psi or -0.93 kg/cm^2) on the container and refill it with the refrigerant you want to transfer.

3.) Container filling operations are controlled by weight. In the shop, containers must be filled to no more than 60% of its gross weight rating. This will prevent overfilling of the container.

5.9 Disposal of Empty or Near-Empty Disposable Containers

Improper scrapping of disposable containers can release some refrigerant into the atmosphere. This must be avoided by removing any of their remaining contents with a recovery or recycling machine as follows:

1.) Attach the service hose of your recovery or recycling machine to the container.

2.) Open the container valve and the recovery/recycling equipment shut-off valve and evacuate the container just as you would a mobile air-conditioning system as previously described in Section 5.2, Refrigerant Recovery Procedure.

3.) When the maximum stable vacuum has been achieved, close the container valve and the service hose shut-off valve, allowing the vacuum to remain in the container.

4.) Mark the container "Empty" and dispose of it properly.

6. Retrofitting CFC-12 (R-12) Mobile Air Conditioning Systems to HFC-134a (R-134a)

6.1 Purpose

This chapter is intended to supplement the vehicle manufacturers' instructions for retrofitting older air-conditioning systems designed for R-12 to the new, ozone-friendly R-134a refrigerant. Following the procedures in this section will help you to comply with SAE standards J1660, Fittings and Labels for Retrofit of CFC-12 (R-12) Mobile Air Conditioning Systems to HFC-134a (R-134a), and J1661, Procedure for Retrofitting CFC-12 (R-12) Mobile Air Conditioning Systems to HFC-134a (R-134a).

Adherence to these standards is important. They provide for a standardized means of retrofitting systems across the auto industry so that any qualified technician can identify and properly service a system that has been retrofitted to use R-134a. The procedures recommended by these standards also provide a means of preparing, cleaning, retrofitting, and charging systems so that the performance and integrity of the air conditioning system is maintained, maximizing your chances of satisfying your customer.

> ### Caution
> Avoid breathing air conditioning refrigerant and lubricant vapor or mist. Exposure may irritate eyes, nose, and throat. The responsible way to avoid this is to use service equipment certified to meet the requirements of SAE J2210 (HFC-134a recycling equipment). SAE J1990 (Extraction and Recycle Equipment for Automotive Air Conditioning Systems) and/or J2209 (Extraction Equipment for Mobile Air Conditioning Systems).

6.2 Applicability

Mobile air-conditioning systems have evolved over time. These procedures can be generally applied to air-conditioning systems that were produced on mid-1980s or newer vehicles.

As with the rest of the SAE standards discussed in this book, this procedure and the SAE standards to which it refers are intended only for air-conditioning systems that are designed to cool the passenger compartment of cars, light trucks, and other vehicles produced with R-12 refrigerant systems similar to those found in passenger cars.

These standards are not applicable to hermetically sealed air-conditioning systems used to refrigerate cargo.

6.3 Retrofit Procedure

6.3.1 Inspection

Check to see if the system has already been retrofitted. A properly retrofitted system will have:

- A sky blue label under the hood that states "Notice: Retrofitted to R-134a." Normally, this label will be placed over or very near the manufacturer's original R-12 label.

- Service ports that are designed to mate with R-134a service equipment. These ports comply with SAE J639. They will be obviously different from the R-12 fittings originally installed. The R-12 fittings will be male fittings with external threads, designed to mate with a hose having a screw-on, flare-type fitting. R-134a fittings will be of the quick disconnect type and may or may not have internal (female) threads used for dust caps.

You can also ask the vehicle owner about the history of the vehicle, perhaps even review AC system service invoices. The owner may be able to tell you that the system has been retrofitted or filled with some other kind of refrigerant. However, the owner may not be completely familiar with the service history of the vehicle. Unless you are absolutely sure that the vehicle has been retrofitted to R-134a, you should assume that it may not have been, and work accordingly.

Use of a refrigerant contamination/identification device may help you to determine the type and purity of the refrigerant in the system (see Chapter 2.3).

6.3.2 Check for System Leaks or Other Problems

1.) Connect an R-12 manifold gauge set to the system. To minimize the escape of R-12 to the atmosphere, be sure that the hoses, shutoff valves, and fittings on the gauge set comply with SAE J2196.

2.) Check the system pressure with the engine and AC fan motor off. If the system has at least 50 psi pressure, check for leaks by following SAE Standard J1628, Leak Test Procedure (See Chapter 2.3). If the system does not have any pressure, or the pressure is very low, recharge the system with R-12 to at least 50 psi (340 kPa). (**Caution:** Leak testing should not be done below 59 °F [15 °C] because even a properly charged system may not have at least 50 psi [340 kPa] pressure.) The purpose of this is to bring the system pressure up high enough to find the leak. However, if there is a major or obvious leak, only charge the system with enough R-12 to find the leak. (Use R-12 recovery or recycling equipment meeting SAE standards J1990 or J2209 as appropriate when adding or removing R-12 from the system at this point in the retrofit procedure.)

3.) If the system is or can be fully charged with R-12 with no major or obvious leaks, test the system performance. Otherwise, perform the necessary repairs to return the system to good mechanical condition and then test the performance.

Check performance by observing high and low side pressures, panel vent air temperatures, and other test indicators recommended by the vehicle manufacturer.

Determine from these tests if any additional repairs are necessary to bring the system up to good mechanical condition. These repairs can be made at the same time that the retrofit modifications are being made (step 8 below).

4.) Recover the R-12 in the system in accordance with SAE Standard J1989 (see chapter 5.2 of this book).

It is vital that all of the R-12 be removed from the system at this step to both ensure that none is released to the atmosphere and that none remains in the system to contaminate the R-134a. There are two precautions you can take to ensure that all the R-12 has been removed:

- During refrigerant recovery, watch the system components, especially the accumulator, and look for frosting. If frosting occurs, gently apply heat to the frosted components to help speed the recovery of the R-12.

- Wait up to five minutes after shutting off the recovery unit before you do anything else. Observe the gauges on your service manifold during this time. If the system pressure is stable for at least two minutes and stays below atmospheric ("0" gauge pressure) for five minutes, it is a good indication that all the refrigerant has been removed.

5.) In most cases the mineral oil lubricant used with R-12 will not be compatible with the R-134a refrigerant. The R-134a will likely require a synthetic lubricant. Refer to the vehicle manufacturer's retrofit instructions to determine if the lubricant must be removed.

To remove the lubricant, drain it from the system, including the compressor, and replace components (such as the drier) that may have lubricant trapped within them, according to the vehicle manufacturer's instructions.

Note: If your repairs include replacing the compressor, be sure to drain the oil from the new compressor unless you are absolutely certain that the oil is compatible with R-134a and the lubricant supplied for the retrofit. Refill the compressor with the specified amount of lubricant compatible with R-134a.

6.) Flush the air conditioning system with R-12 to clean out any remaining contaminants. Because you will likely be changing the type of lubricant in the system, the flushing equipment you use must be of the type that separates the lubricant from the R-12 flushing agent. Flushing is accomplished by following the manufacturer's instructions which usually include:

- Prepare the system for flushing by opening the system at appropriate points to provide an inlet and an outlet for the R-12.

- Connect both a vacuum pump and flushing equipment to the system or component so that the system or component can be evacuated and then flushed without again opening the system to the atmosphere. Be sure all connections are leak-tight.

- Evacuate the system or component being flushed in order to avoid contaminating the R-12 flushing equipment.

- Flush the system with R-12 for the time recommended by the vehicle manufacturer.

- Be sure to cleanse the R-12 used as a flushing agent to at least the level of purity required by SAE J1991 before again using it.

- Completely recover the R-12 used as a flushing agent from the system by following the procedures outlined in Chapter 5.2. Remember that the flushing process has completely filled the system or component with liquid R-12. It is therefore very important to monitor all system components for frosting, which is even more likely to occur in system that has been completely filled with liquid R-12. As before, gently apply heat to frosted components to aid in the recovery of all the R-12.

7.) Remove all of the R-12 service equipment. You will not need it again for this vehicle.

8.) Make the necessary mechanical repairs and changes to the system. These will include:

- Repairs you found necessary in step 4, above, as well as changing any components required by the vehicle manufacturer's retrofit procedure. These components may include hoses, oil seals, and the drier (desiccant) as well as a change in or addition of a compressor shutoff switch.

- Addition of the required amount and type of lubricant in the manner recommended by the vehicle manufacturer. Because the system has been flushed, be sure to add lubricant directly into the compressor crankcase or the low-side service port near the compressor to ensure proper compressor lubrication at start-up.

> **Caution**
> Lubricants for mobile air-conditioning systems using R-134a may damage the appearance of painted surfaces and plastic parts. Avoid spilling the lubricant on these surfaces.

- Change refrigerant service ports to those for R-134a in accordance with SAE standards J1660 and J639. R-134a service ports are quick-disconnect-type fittings. (They may also have internal [female] threads for holding a dust cap.) The proper retrofit R-134a service ports will either convert the R-12 service ports irreversibly to R-134a connections, or will add R-134a service ports. If the R-134a service ports do not alter the R-12 ports, the R-12 ports must be made unusable by adding a plug or cap that is installed with thread-lock adhesive or a mechanical locking device (snap ring, drive-wire, roll-pin, or non-removable plug) that discourages removal.

- Installation of a label that states: "Notice: Retrofitted to R-134a" and "Retrofit procedure performed to SAE (standard) J1661" on top of the original R-12 label. Be sure that the new label does not obscure non-R-12 specific information about the air-conditioning system. All labels used must meet SAE standard J1660 to ensure durability, completeness, and clarity.

  To meet SAE standards, this label must have a sky-blue background and shall also include information on the amount of R-134a refrigerant that is supposed to be charged into the system and the required lubricant amount and type. It must also include your name and address or the name and address of the shop that performed the retrofit.

  If a single label that contains all of the above information is too big to fit over the original R-12 information without obscuring other, non-R-12 information, an auxiliary label may be used. The R-12 data (only) must be obliterated in an irreversible manner, which could include covering with a smaller label that indicates the location of the auxiliary label. The auxiliary label must also have a sky-blue background and be installed in an easily accessible part or surface not normally replaced during vehicle service or accident repair.

  If the retrofit label cannot be placed directly over the existing R-12 information, it must be placed as closely as possible to the R-12 label. The original R-12 information, and only the R-12 information, must be permanently obliterated.

9.) You are now ready to evacuate the system and then install the proper amount of R-134a. Connect hoses from the manifold gauge set or the R-134a charging equipment to the air conditioning system service ports.

10.) Use a vacuum pump dedicated for R-134a and having R-134a fittings (per SAE J2197) to evacuate the system. The vacuum pump may be part of the R-134a recycling or extraction equipment. The purpose of doing this is to remove air and any remaining traces of R-12. Excess R-12 levels may cause chemical contamination and system damage.

To ensure all R-12 has been removed, evacuate the system for at least 30 minutes (45 minutes for systems with dual evaporators such as those with front and rear evaporators). The vacuum pump must be capable of pulling the system down to a vacuum level of 2.7 kPa (29.2 inches of mercury), adjusted for altitude.

11.) Check the system for leaks by isolating the vacuum pump from the system and watching for any change in pressure. If the pressure rises, find and repair the leak.

Caution

Do not pressure test or leak test R-134a (HFC-134a) service equipment and/or vehicle air conditioning systems with compressed air. Some mixtures of air and HFC-134a have been shown to be combustible at elevated pressures. These mixtures, if ignited, may cause injury or property damage. Additional health and safety information may be obtained from refrigerant manufacturers and/or on the Material Safety Data Sheets.

After fixing the leak, evacuate the system again for 15 minutes and then again check for leaks. If the system is leak-tight, move on to the next step. If it still will not hold a vacuum, find and repair the leak, and then repeat the vacuum test.

12.) Charge the air conditioning system with R-134a in the amount and manner recommended by the vehicle manufacturer. Do NOT use the sight glass to determine the proper charge level. R-134a has characteristics that will give you a false sight glass reading. Bubbles may or may not be an indication of an undercharged system. Residual mineral oil may also be swept up by the R-134a and produce milky white streaks in the sight glass, obscuring your view.

13.) Ensure that all hoses and service equipment, tools, and other equipment are clear of the engine belts and other moving parts.

14.) Operate the air conditioning system and determine that it is operating properly. Do this by checking pressure levels, inlet and outlet temperatures, or other parameters specified by the vehicle manufacturer for the retrofitted system. (**Note:** The acceptable values for these parameters may be different than those for the system operating on R-12.)

15.) Shut off the system and the vehicle, disconnect all the service equipment and fit the caps and seals on to all the service ports.

16.) Conduct a final leak check in accordance with Chapter 2.3 (SAE standard J1628) using a leak detector compatible with R-134a. If any leaks are found, reconnect your R-134a service equipment, extract the refrigerant, and repair the system.

Appendix A

Applicable SAE Standards

The following standards are included in this Appendix:

- J639   Safety and Containment of Refrigerant for Mechanical Vapor Compression Systems used for Mobile Air-Conditioning Systems

- J1628   Technician Procedure for Using Electronic Refrigerant Leak Detectors for Service of Mobile Air Conditoning Systems

- J1629   Cautionary Statements for Handling HFC-134a During Mobile Air Conditioning Service

- J1660   Fittings and Lables for Retrofit of CFC-12 (R-12) Mobile Air Conditioning Systems to HFC-134a (R-134a)

- J1661   Procedure for Retrofitting CFC-12 (R-12) Mobile Air Conditioning Systems to HFC-134a (R-134a)

- J1989   Recommended Service Procedure for the Containment of R-12

- J1991   Standard of Purity for Use in Mobile Air-Conditioning Systems

- J2099   Standard of Purity for Recycled HFC-134a For Use in Mobile Air-Conditioning Systems

- J2196   Service Hose for Automotive Air Conditioning

- J2197   HFC-134a Service Hose Fittings for Automotive Air-Conditioning Service Equipment

- J2211   Recommended Service Procedure for the Containment of HFC-134a

- J2219   Concern to the Mobile Air-Conditioning Industry

Related SAE standards include:

- J1990   Extraction and Recycle Equipment for Mobile Automotive Air-Conditioning Systems

J2209   CFC-12 Extraction Equipment for Mobile Automotive Air-Conditioning Systems

J2210   HFC-134a Recycling Equipment for Mobile Air-Conditioning Systems

These and other SAE standards may be obtained from:

>SAE Customer Sales & Satisfaction
>400 Commonwealth Drive
>Warrendale, PA 15096-0001
>(412) 776-4970

SAE *The Engineering Society For Advancing Mobility Land Sea Air and Space®* *I N T E R N A T I O N A L* 400 Commonwealth Drive, Warrendale, PA 15096-0001	**SURFACE VEHICLE RECOMMENDED PRACTICE** Submitted for recognition as an American National Standard	**SAE** J639	**REV. APR94** Issued 1953-04 Revised 1994-04-26 Superseding J639 NOV91

SAFETY AND CONTAINMENT OF REFRIGERANT FOR MECHANICAL VAPOR COMPRESSION SYSTEMS USED FOR MOBILE AIR-CONDITIONING SYSTEMS

1. Scope—This SAE Recommended Practice is restricted to mechanical vapor compression refrigerant systems driven by the vehicle or auxiliary engine, which provides cooling for the passenger compartment. This document provides guidelines for refrigerant containment and safety for a mobile air-conditioning system. It is not intended to restrict the use of, or further development of, other types of refrigeration systems for passenger compartment cooling. Should other systems be found practical at some future time, this document may be amended or an additional recommended safety practice drawn up for such other systems.

2 References

2.1 Applicable Documents—The following publication forms a part of this specification to the extent specified herein. The latest issue of SAE Publications shall apply.

(R) 2.1.1 SAE Publication—Available from SAE, 400 Commonwealth Drive, Warrendale, PA 15096-0001.

SAE J2197—HFC-134a (R134a) Service Hose Fittings for Automotive Air-Conditioning Service Equipment

(R) 2.1.2 ASHRAE Publication—Available from ASHRAE, 17191 Tullie Circle NE, Atlanta, GA 30329-2305.

ASHRAE 34-1992—Number Designation and Safety Classification of Refrigerants

3. Components—A mechanical vapor compression refrigeration system for cooling the passenger compartment of a motor vehicle consists of:

a. A pump or compressor which raises the pressure of the refrigerant vapor and in so doing also raises its temperature.
b. A condenser where the compressed refrigerant vapor is cooled and liquefied by passing outside air over its surface to absorb heat from the refrigerant.
c. An expansion valve or other liquid refrigerant metering device regulates the flow of refrigerant to the evaporator.
d. An evaporator, wherein the liquid refrigerant vaporizes because of the heat which it absorbs from the air passing over the evaporator surface.
e. A blower unit which circulates air over the evaporator where the air is cooled and then delivered to the passenger compartment. The air which is supplied to the evaporator unit may come from the passenger compartment (recirculated air), from the outside of the vehicle (outside air), or as a mixture of recirculated and outside air.

SAE Technical Standards Board Rules provide that: "This report is published by SAE to advance the state of technical and engineering sciences. The use of this report is entirely voluntary, and its applicability and suitability for any particular use, including any patent infringement arising therefrom, is the sole responsibility of the user."

SAE reviews each technical report at least every five years at which time it may be reaffirmed, revised, or cancelled. SAE invites your written comments and suggestions.

Copyright 1994 Society of Automotive Engineers, Inc.
All rights reserved.   Printed in U.S.A.

SAE J639 Revised APR94

    f. A system of controls which may be manual, automatic, or part manual and part automatic. The control elements may control air delivery by the evaporator unit, temperature in the passenger compartment, the amount of outside air introduced, maximum pressure within the system, and similar items.

    g. In addition, the system may require wiring, tubing, connections, air ducts, a means of driving the compressor and the evaporator blower, a means of cooling the condenser, and other components.

4. *Refrigerants*—The refrigerant must be of low toxicity, nonflammable, and nonexplosive, such as CFC-12, HFC-22, HFC-134a, as defined by the American Society of Heating, Refrigeration, and Air Conditioning Engineers in ASHRAE 34-1992. Blend refrigerants, both in the original composition and in compositions created as a result of normal mobile air-conditioning operating conditions, must meet the previous criteria: low toxicity, nonflammable, and nonexplosive requirements.

5. *Safety Practices*—The following safety practices are recommended:

5.1 A pressure-sensitive relief device shall be located in the high-pressure side of the compressor or immediately adjacent to the compressor discharge port. The device shall be vented to the outside of the passenger and baggage compartments and air-circulating system for the passenger compartment. In no case shall the release (blow off) pressure be greater than 4136 kPa (600 psig) with any refrigerant.

5.2 The high-pressure side of the system components shall have an ultimate bursting pressure not less than two times the release pressure as established in 5.1.

5.3 To avoid the connection of a low-pressure container or service equipment to the high-pressure side of the system, any service fitting which connects into the high-pressure side refrigerant passage shall be mechanically dissimilar from the low-pressure side service fitting. The service fittings shall only be used to access the system for service and should be located for easy access. High- and low-side service fittings including protective or sealing caps shall provide containment of the refrigerant equal to the design intent "point" leakage rate of the system.

5.3.1 To prevent mixing of CFC-12 and HFC-134a refrigerants in mobile air-conditioning systems, Figure 1 illustrates the low-pressure fitting and Figure 2 illustrates the high-pressure fitting for CFC-12. Figure 3 illustrates the low-pressure fitting and Figure 4 illustrates the high-pressure fitting for HFC-134a. The internal threads are optional for sealing caps as required in 5.3. No external threads shall be allowed on the fittings in Figures 3 and 4.

(R)   *5.3.1.1* Charge couplings used in conjunction with fittings in Figures 3 and 4 shall have a relief feature to prevent coupling blow-off during installation and removal. The coupler depressor shall have a concave radius and shall provide a self-alignment feature. The coupling depressor travel, which depresses the pneumatic valve core (which shall have a pin convex radius of 1.9 mm, Figure 5), has a pin location at breach of seal of 6.1 mm to 7.1 mm from the face of the fitting. (Breach of seal means when valve starts to open.) Minimum depressor travel must be 7.8 mm and to prevent core pin damage due to over-travel, the maximum coupling depression location shall not exceed 8.3 mm from the face of the fitting noted in Figures 3 and 4. Charge couplings shall open the service hose to flow only on mandatory dimensioned features shown in Figures 3 and 4.

(R)   *5.3.1.2* For clearance during installation, the service fitting access coupler shall have a minimum inside diameter of 16.20 mm for the high side and 13.20 mm for the low side as identified in Figures 3 and 4. These requirements are to insure proper installation and retention of the coupler during mobile air-conditioning service operation. The coupler shall also conform to the appropriate requirements in SAE J2197.

SAE J639 Revised APR94

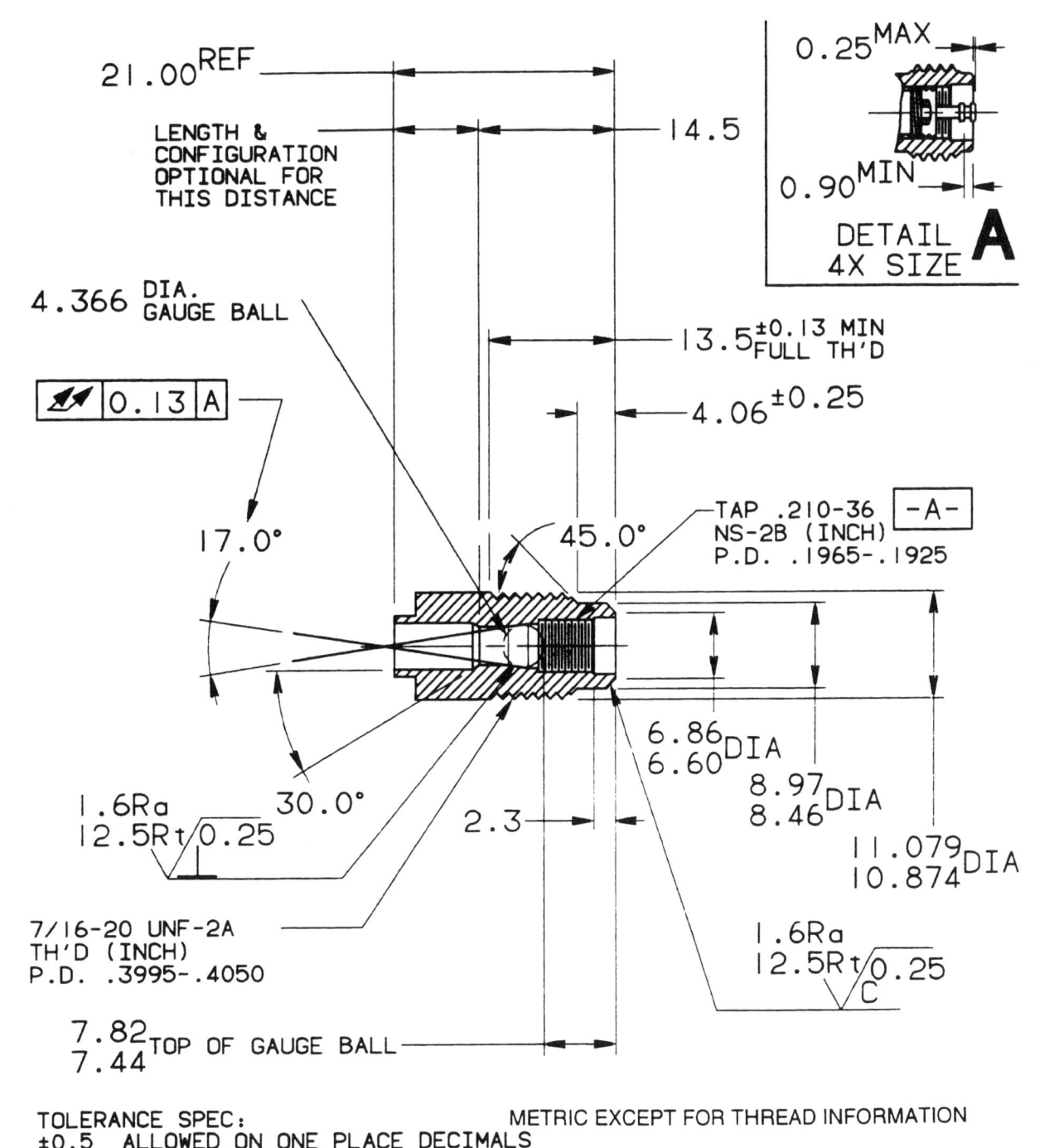

(R) FIGURE 1—CFC-12 LOW-PRESSURE SERVICE VALVE FITTING

- 21.00 REF
- LENGTH & CONFIGURATION OPTIONAL FOR THIS DISTANCE
- 14.5
- 4.366 DIA. GAUGE BALL
- 13.5 ±0.13 MIN FULL TH'D
- 4.06 ±0.25
- 0.13 A
- 17.0°
- 45.0°
- TAP .210-36 NS-2B (INCH) -A-
  P.D. .1965-.1925
- 30.0°
- 1.6 Ra
- 12.5 Rt / 0.25
- 2.3
- 6.86 / 6.60 DIA
- 8.97 / 8.46 DIA
- 11.079 / 10.874 DIA
- 7/16-20 UNF-2A TH'D (INCH)
  P.D. .3995-.4050
- 1.6 Ra
- 12.5 Rt / 0.25 C
- 7.82 / 7.44 TOP OF GAUGE BALL

DETAIL A 4X SIZE
- 0.25 MAX
- 0.90 MIN

TOLERANCE SPEC:
±0.5 ALLOWED ON ONE PLACE DECIMALS
±0.25 ALLOWED ON TWO PLACE DECIMALS
±5.0° ALLOWED ON ANGLES UNLESS OTHERWISE SPECIFIED
ALL ANGLES 45.0° UNLESS OTHERWISE SPECIFIED

METRIC EXCEPT FOR THREAD INFORMATION

SAE J639 Revised APR94

21.00 REF

LENGTH & CONFIGURATION OPTIONAL FOR THIS DISTANCE

14.5

0.25 MAX
0.90 MIN

DETAIL A
4X SIZE

4.366 DIA GAUGE BALL

9.91 ±0.13 MIN FULL TH'D

3.05 ±0.25

⌿ 0.13 A

TAP .210-36 NS-2B (INCH)
P.D. .1965-.1925
-A-

9.60 / 7.37 DIA

45.0°

17.0°

30.0°

5.92 / 5.66 DIA

6.91 / 5.66 DIA

8.13 / 7.42 DIA

1.6 Ra
12.5 Rt / 0.25
C

1.6 Ra
12.5 Rt / 0.25

2.3

7.82 / 7.44 TOP OF GAUGE BALL

8.60 / 7.80

3/8-24 UNF-2A TH'D (INCH)
P.D. .3479-.3430

METRIC EXCEPT FOR THREAD INFORMATION

TOLERANCE SPEC:
±0.5   ALLOWED ON ONE PLACE DECIMALS
±0.25 ALLOWED ON TWO PLACE DECIMALS
±5.0° ALLOWED ON ANGLES UNLESS OTHERWISE SPECIFIED
ALL ANGLES 45.0° UNLESS OTHERWISE SPECIFIED

(R) FIGURE 2—CFC-12 HIGH-PRESSURE SERVICE VALVE FITTING

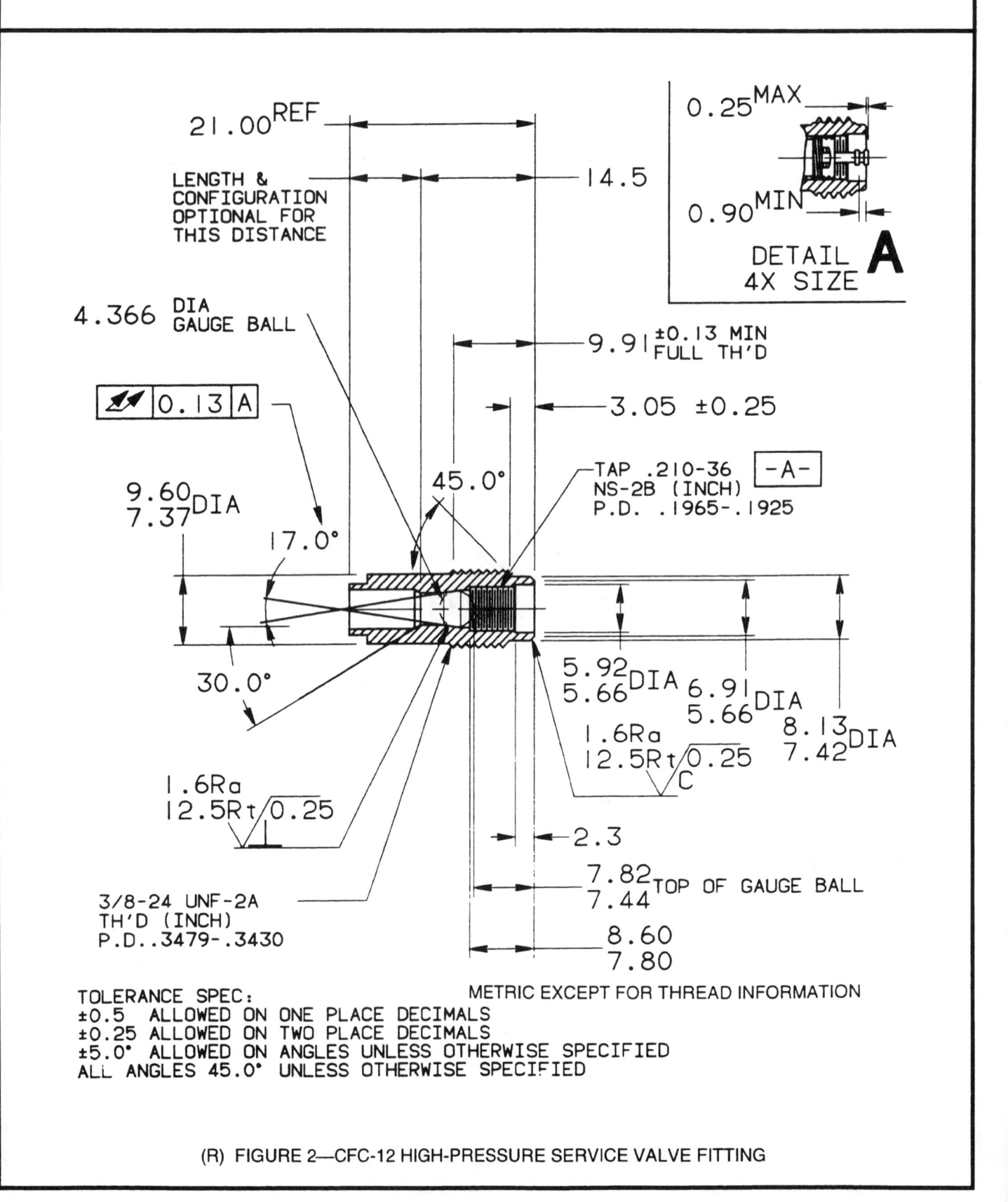

SAE J639 Revised APR94

FIGURE 3—LOW SIDE FOR HFC-134a SERVICE VALVE FITTING

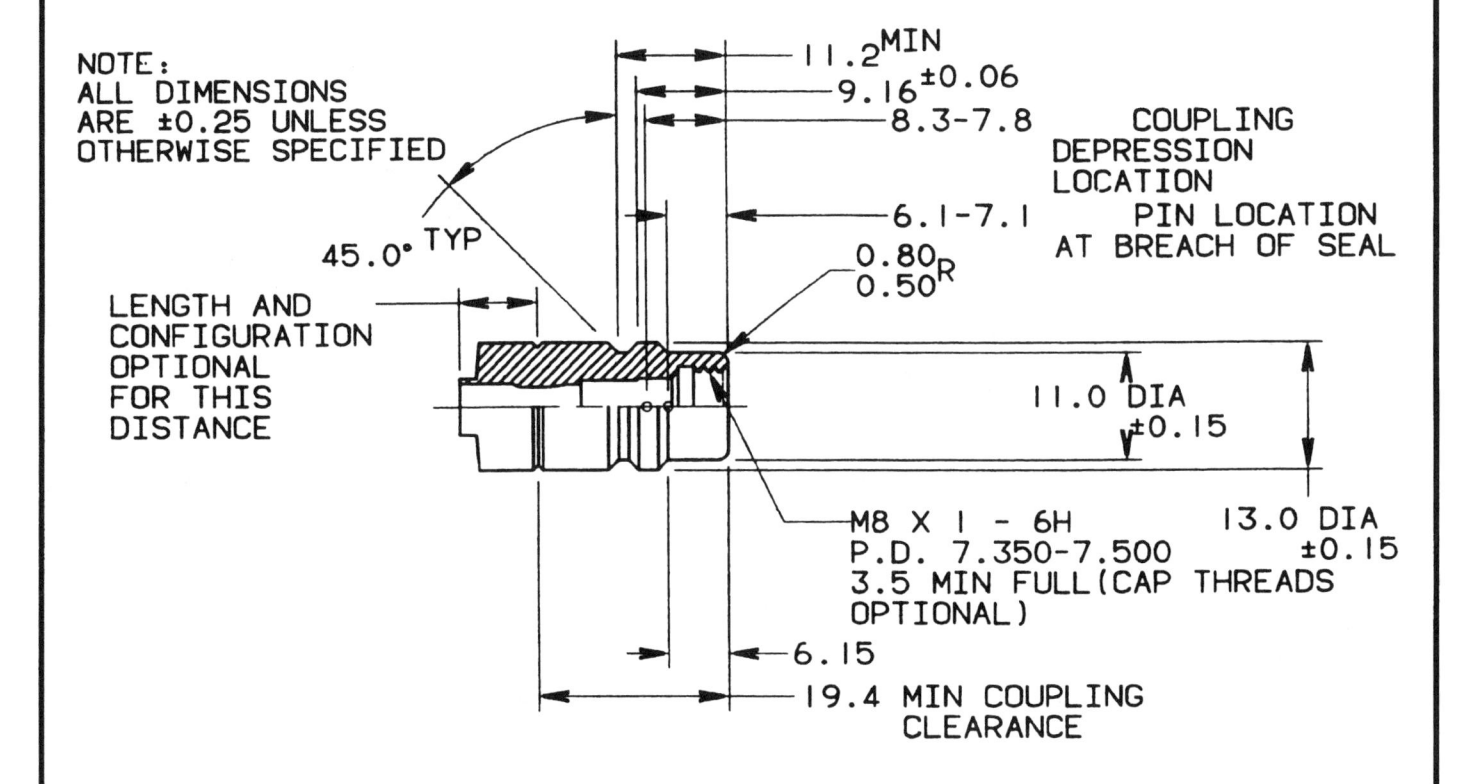

Dimensions are metric

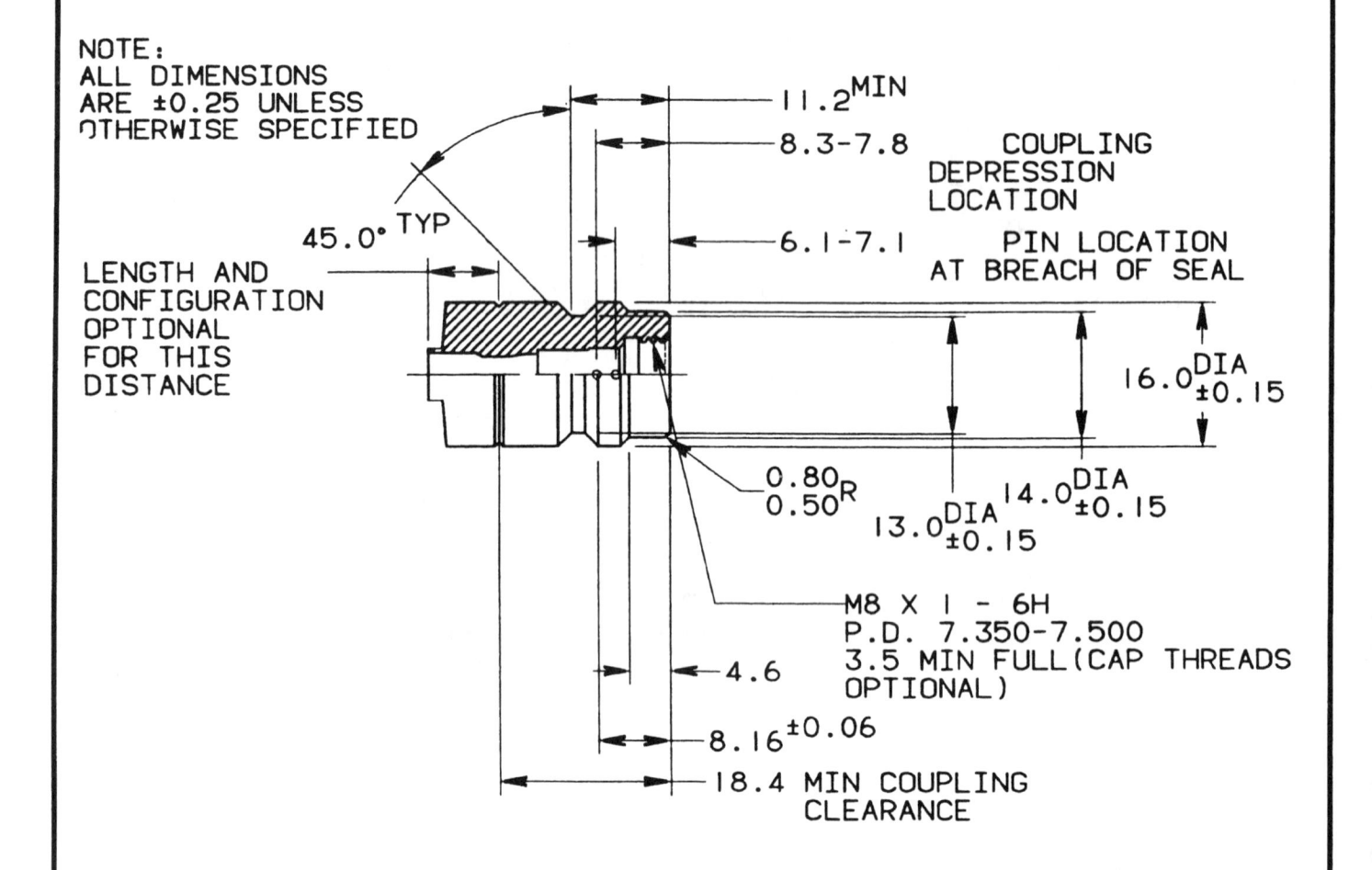

SAE J639 Revised APR94

NOTE:
ALL DIMENSIONS
ARE ±0.25 UNLESS
OTHERWISE SPECIFIED

11.2 MIN

8.3-7.8 COUPLING DEPRESSION LOCATION

6.1-7.1 PIN LOCATION AT BREACH OF SEAL

45.0° TYP

LENGTH AND
CONFIGURATION
OPTIONAL
FOR THIS
DISTANCE

16.0 DIA ±0.15

0.80 R
0.50 R

14.0 DIA ±0.15

13.0 DIA ±0.15

M8 X 1 - 6H
P.D. 7.350-7.500
3.5 MIN FULL (CAP THREADS OPTIONAL)

4.6

8.16 ±0.06

18.4 MIN COUPLING CLEARANCE

Dimensions are metric

(R) FIGURE 4—HIGH SIDE FOR HFC-134a SERVICE VALVE FITTING

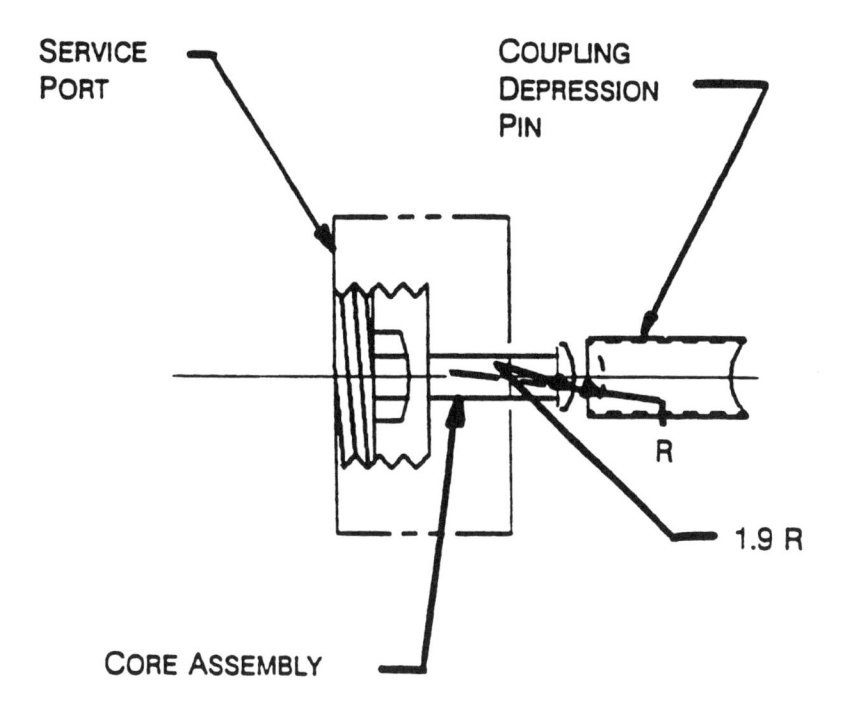

FIGURE 5—PIN CONVEX RADIUS OF 1.9 mm

6. Design Practice

6.1 A plainly legible and durable name plate or tag shall be mounted in the engine compartment, such as on a body structure part or air-conditioning component, not normally replaced during service or vehicle accident damage replacement, where it can be easily seen. The name plate or tag shall include identification of the refrigerant and lubricant type and the recommended amount of refrigerant charge. The name plate or tag shall show the name and address of the refrigeration system manufacturer or the merchandiser responsible for design compliance with this document. It shall also reference appropriate repair practices. The plate or tag shall also state: CAUTION—SYSTEM TO BE SERVICED BY QUALIFIED PERSONNEL.

6.2 The type of refrigerant and recommended system charge amount, lubricant type, shall be identified in the vehicle owner's manual.

6.3 To provide containment and prevent discharge of refrigerant during system operation, the system shall have a device which limits the compressor operation before the pressure relief device in 5.1 will vent refrigerant.

7. Notes

7.1 Marginal Indicia—The (R) is for the convenience of the user in locating areas where technical revisions have been made to the previous issue of the report. If the symbol is next to the report title, it indicates a complete revision of the report.

PREPARED BY THE SAE INTERIOR CLIMATE CONTROL STANDARDS COMMITTEE

SAE The Engineering Society For Advancing Mobility Land Sea Air and Space® INTERNATIONAL 400 Commonwealth Drive, Warrendale, PA 15096-0001	**SURFACE VEHICLE STANDARD**	SAE J1628
		Issued 1993-06-02
	Submitted for recognition as an American National Standard	

TECHNICIAN PROCEDURE FOR USING ELECTRONIC REFRIGERANT LEAK DETECTORS FOR SERVICE OF MOBILE AIR CONDITIONING SYSTEMS

Foreword—The purpose of this SAE Recommended Practice is to establish minimum standard practices for service leak detection of motor vehicle passenger compartment air conditioning systems. After exhaustive review of electronic leak detection methods in use today, the following has been proven a reliable means of detecting refrigerant leaks.

1. *Scope*—This SAE Recommended Practice applies to the use of generally available electronic leak detection methods to service motor vehicle passenger compartment air conditioning systems.

2. *References*

2.1 **Applicable Documents**—The following publication forms a part of this specification to the extent specified herein. The latest issue of SAE publications shall apply.

2.1.1 SAE PUBLICATION—Available from SAE, 400 Commonwealth Drive, Warrendale, PA 15096-0001.

SAE J1627—Rating Criteria for Electronic Refrigerant Leak Detectors

3. *Electronic Probe-Type Detector Instructions*

3.1 The electronic leak detector shall be operated in accordance with the equipment manufacturer's operating instructions.

3.2 Leak test with the engine not in operation.

3.3 The air conditioning system shall be charged with sufficient refrigerant to have a gauge pressure of at least 340 kPa (50 psi) when not in operation. At temperatures below 15 °C (59 °F), leaks may not be measurable, since this pressure may not be reached.

3.4 Take care not to contaminate the detector probe tip if the part being tested is contaminated. If the part is particularly dirty, it should be wiped off with a dry shop towel or blown off with shop air. No cleaners or solvents shall be used, since many electronic detectors are sensitive to their ingredients.

SAE Technical Standards Board Rules provide that: "This report is published by SAE to advance the state of technical and engineering sciences. The use of this report is entirely voluntary, and its applicability and suitability for any particular use, including any patent infringement arising therefrom, is the sole responsibility of the user."

SAE reviews each technical report at least every five years at which time it may be reaffirmed, revised, or cancelled. SAE invites your written comments and suggestions.

Copyright 1993 Society of Automotive Engineers, Inc.
All rights reserved.

SAE J1628 Issued JUN93

3.5 Visually trace the entire refrigerant system, and look for signs of air conditioning lubricant leakage, damage, and corrosion on all lines, hoses, and components. Each questionable area shall be carefully checked with the detector probe, as well as all fittings, hose to line couplings, refrigerant controls, service ports with caps in place, brazed or welded areas, and areas around attachment points and hold-downs on lines and components.

3.6 Always follow the refrigerant system around in a continuous path so that no areas of potential leaks are missed. If a leak is found, always continue to test the remainder of the system.

3.7 At each area checked, the probe shall be moved around the location, at a rate no more than 25 to 50 mm/s (1 to 2 in/s), and no more than 5 mm (1/4 in) from the surface completely around the position. Slower and closer movement of the probe greatly improves the likelihood of finding a leak.

3.8 An apparent leak shall be verified at least once by blowing shop air into the area of the suspected leak, if necessary, and repeating the check of the area. In cases of very large leaks, blowing out the area with shop air often helps locate the exact position of the leak.

3.9 Leak testing of the evaporator core while in the air conditioning module shall be accomplished by turning the air conditioning blower on high for a period of 15 s minimum, shutting it off, then waiting for the refrigerant to accumulate in the case for time specified by 3.9.1, then inserting the leak detector probe into the blower resistor block or condensate drain hole if no water is present, or into the closest opening in the heating/ventilation/air conditioning case to the evaporator, such as the heater duct or a vent duct. If the detector alarms, a leak apparently has been found.

3.9.1 The accumulation time shall be specified by the leak detector manufacturer in the instructions included with the detector.

3.10 Following any service to the refrigerant system of the vehicle, and any other service which disturbs the refrigerant system, a leak test of the repair and of the service ports of the refrigerant system shall be done.

PREPARED BY THE SAE INTERIOR CLIMATE CONTROL STANDARDS COMMITTEE

SAE International 400 Commonwealth Drive, Warrendale, PA 15096-0001	**SURFACE VEHICLE INFORMATION REPORT**	SAE J1629 Issued 1993-06-02

CAUTIONARY STATEMENTS FOR HANDLING HFC-134a DURING MOBILE AIR CONDITIONING SERVICE

Foreword—The purpose of this SAE Information Report is to provide cautionary statements for the mobile air conditioning industry to alert service technicians to the inadvisability and the possible health and safety effects associated with (a) venting HFC-134a (R-134a) systems to the atmosphere, and (b) using compressed air for leak detection in HFC-134a systems during service operations.

1. Scope

1.1 The cautionary statements presented in this SAE Information Report are to be included in all current and future SAE standards involving service practices (J2211) and service equipment (J2210) for HFC-134a refrigerant.

1.2 It is also intended that these cautionary statements (or equivalent language) be recommended for inclusion in all publications dealing with the servicing of HFC-134a mobile air conditioning systems.

2. References

2.1 Applicable Documents—The following publications form a part of this specification to the extent specified herein. The latest issue of SAE publications shall apply.

2.1.1 SAE PUBLICATIONS—Available from SAE, 400 Commonwealth Drive, Warrendale, PA 15096-0001.

SAE J2210—HFC-134a Recycling Equipment for Mobile Air Conditioning Systems
SAE J2211—Recommended Service Procedures for the Containment of HFC-134a

3. Cautionary Statements

3.1 Caution—Avoid breathing air conditioning refrigerant and lubricant vapor or mist. Exposure may irritate eyes, nose, and throat. To remove HFC-134a from the air conditioning system, use service equipment certified to meet the requirements of SAE J2210 (HFC-134a recycling equipment). Additional health and safety information may be obtained from refrigerant and lubricant manufacturers.

3.2 Caution—Do not pressure test or leak test HFC-134a service equipment and/or vehicle air conditioning systems with compressed air. Some mixtures of air and HFC-134a have been shown to be combustible at elevated pressures. These mixtures, if ignited, may cause injury or property damage. Additional health and safety information may be obtained from refrigerant manufacturers.

PREPARED BY THE SAE INTERIOR CLIMATE CONTROL STANDARDS COMMITTEE

SAE Technical Standards Board Rules provide that: "This report is published by SAE to advance the state of technical and engineering sciences. The use of this report is entirely voluntary, and its applicability and suitability for any particular use, including any patent infringement arising therefrom, is the sole responsibility of the user."

SAE reviews each technical report at least every five years at which time it may be reaffirmed, revised, or cancelled. SAE invites your written comments and suggestions.

Copyright 1993 Society of Automotive Engineers, Inc.
All rights reserved.

SAE The Engineering Society For Advancing Mobility Land Sea Air and Space

INTERNATIONAL

400 Commonwealth Drive, Warrendale, PA 15096-0001

SURFACE VEHICLE RECOMMENDED PRACTICE

Submitted for recognition as an American National Standard

SAE J1660

Issued 1993-06-02

FITTINGS AND LABELS FOR RETROFIT OF CFC-12 (R12) MOBILE AIR CONDITIONING SYSTEMS TO HFC-134a (R134a)

1. *Scope*—This SAE Recommended Practice describes the specific measures required to meet SAE established criteria when retrofitting CFC-12 (R12) mobile air conditioning systems to HFC-134a (R134a), with regards to fittings and labeling. This document is complete only when combined with the requirements of SAE J1657.

2. *References*

2.1 **Applicable Documents**—The following publications form a part of this specification to the extent specified herein. The latest issue of SAE publications shall apply.

2.1.1 SAE PUBLICATIONS—Available from SAE, 400 Commonwealth Drive, Warrendale, PA 15096-0001.

SAE J639—Safety and Containment of Refrigerant for Vapor Compression Systems for Mobile Air Conditioning Systems
SAE J1627—Rating Criteria for Electronic Refrigerant Leak Detectors
SAE J1628—Technician Procedure for Using Electronic Refrigerant Leak Detector for Service of Mobile Air Conditioning Systems
SAE J1657—Selection Criteria for Retrofit Refrigerants to Replace CFC-12 (R12) in Mobile Air Conditioning Systems
SAE J1661—Procedure for Retrofitting CFC-12 (R12) Mobile Air Conditioning Systems to HFC-134a (R134a)
SAE J2064—R-134a Refrigerant Automotive Air Conditioning Hose

2.1.2 UL PUBLICATION—Available from Underwriters Laboratories, Inc., 333 Pfingsten Road, Northbrook, IL 60062-2096.

ANSI/UL 969-1991—Marking and Labeling Systems

3. *Fittings*

3.1 There shall be at least one system service port which complies with SAE J639 for R134a. If both a high side and low side service port exist, there shall be at least one high side and at least one low side system service port which complies with SAE J639 for R134a after the retrofit is completed.

SAE Technical Standards Board Rules provide that: "This report is published by SAE to advance the state of technical and engineering sciences. The use of this report is entirely voluntary, and its applicability and suitability for any particular use, including any patent infringement arising therefrom, is the sole responsibility of the user."

SAE reviews each technical report at least every five years at which time it may be reaffirmed, revised, or cancelled. SAE invites your written comments and suggestions.

Copyright 1993 Society of Automotive Engineers, Inc.
All rights reserved.

SAE J1660 Issued JUN93

3.2 When existing R12 service ports are to be retrofit, R134a conversion assemblies shall be fitted. The conversion assembly shall attach to the R12 fitting with a thread lock adhesive and/or a separate mechanical latching mechanism (e.g., snap-ring, drive-wire, roll pin, etc.) in a manner that prevents the assembly from being removed inadvertently.

3.2.1 A conversion assembly that consists of flexible portion(s) as well as nonflexible couplings and/or fittings shall comply with SAE J639. Such a conversion assembly, up to and including the appropriate R12 interface, shall be considered a hose assembly and shall meet all requirements of SAE J2064. Such a conversion assembly shall also meet the following vibration test requirements. Following successful completion of the SAE J2064 Coupling Integrity Test, subject these same test specimen assemblies, still charged with the appropriate amount of refrigerant (5.3.2.1), to the following vibration testing sequence:

a. Install each test specimen assembly on a vibration table with the conversion adaptor positioned downward.
b. Expose the assembly to 77 °C + 5 °C and vibrate at 30 Hz + 5 Hz and 1.57 mm total displacement in a vertical direction for 200 h followed by 200 h in a horizontal direction.

At the end of test, verify gravimetrically that the test assembly still has a refrigerant charge. Refrigerant leakage at the end of test shall not exceed 0.45 kg per 40 years. Leak detection equipment and methodology shall conform to SAE J1627 and J1628.

3.2.2 A conversion assembly that consists solely of nonflexible couplings and/or fittings shall comply with SAE J639. Such a conversion assembly, up to and including the appropriate R12 interface, shall be tested in accordance with SAE J2064 Coupling Integrity Testing sections covering coupling integrity, test specimens, charging and exposure, after which refrigerant leakage shall not exceed 0.45 kg per 40 years. Leak detection equipment and methodology shall conform to SAE J1627 and J1628. Following successful completion of this "modified" SAE J2064 Coupling Integrity Test, subject these same test specimen assemblies, still charged with the appropriate amount of refrigerant, to the following vibration testing sequence.

a. Install each test specimen assembly on a vibration table with the conversion adaptor position downward.
b. Expose the assembly to 77 °C + 5 °C and vibrate at 30 Hz + 5 Hz and 1.57 mm total displacement in a vertical direction for 200 h followed by 200 h in a horizontal direction.

Refrigerant leakage at the end of test shall not exceed 0.45 kg per 40 years. Leak detection equipment and methodology shall conform to SAE J1627 and J1628.

3.2.3 Only a conversion assembly meeting the requirements of 3.2.1 and 3.2.2 may be labeled with "SAE J1660" or "Complies with SAE J1660."

3.3 When new R134a service ports are added, they shall conform to SAE J639. Such added retrofit service ports shall comply with SAE J2064 Coupling Integrity Test 5.3.2 and 5.3.3.

3.4 All R12 service ports shall either be retrofitted with conversion assemblies as in 3.2, or be rendered incompatible with R12 related service equipment by fitting with a device such as a plug or cap. This device shall attach to the R12 fitting with a thread locking adhesive and/or a separate latching mechanism (e.g., snap-ring, drive-wire, roll pin, nonremovable plug) that prevents the device from being removed inadvertently.

4. *Labels*—When a retrofit procedure is performed, a label(s) documenting the change shall be affixed to the vehicle as described as follows.

4.1 The retrofit label shall have a header with the words "NOTICE: RETROFITTED TO R134a."

4.1.1 The background color of the retrofit label shall be PMS 2975, Sky Blue.

SAE J1660 Issued JUN93

4.1.2 The retrofit label shall comply with SAE J639. The retrofit label material and construction shall conform to all specifications and requirements appropriate for the intended installed location, i.e., a decal installed in the engine compartment shall meet temperature requirements. Testing of decals shall meet ANSI/UL 969-1991.

4.1.3 The retrofit label shall contain "Retrofit procedure performed to SAE J1661," as well as the refrigerant charge amount and lubricant type.

4.1.4 The retrofit label shall be affixed over the existing R12 label, provided this does not limit visibility of other information unrelated to R12. In any case, the retrofit label shall be affixed as close to the original R12 label as possible, on an easily accessible part or surface not normally replaced during service or vehicle accident damage replacement.

4.1.5 All information related to R12 on existing labels shall be rendered unreadable by some permanent means, such as complete removal, sectioning, tamper-proof masking, permanent marking, or overlay by the retrofit label.

4.1.6 The retrofit label, or the auxiliary label described in 4.2, shall contain the name and address of the company or individual who performed the retrofit, the date of the retrofit, type and amount of refrigerant, and type and amount of lubricant used. If an auxiliary label is used, the retrofit label shall contain the location of the auxiliary label.

4.2 An auxiliary label shall be required if the retrofit label does not contain all the information required in 4.1.

4.2.1 The background color of the auxiliary label shall be PMS 2975, Sky Blue.

4.2.2 The auxiliary label material and construction shall conform to all specifications and requirements appropriate for the intended installed location, i.e., a decal installed in the engine compartment shall meet temperature requirements. Testing of decals shall meet ANSI/UL 969-1991. The auxiliary label shall be affixed in an easily accessible location on a part or surface not normally replaced during service.

PREPARED BY THE SAE INTERIOR CLIMATE CONTROL STANDARDS COMMITTEE

SAE *The Engineering Society For Advancing Mobility Land Sea Air and Space*

INTERNATIONAL

400 Commonwealth Drive, Warrendale, PA 15096-0001

SURFACE VEHICLE RECOMMENDED PRACTICE

Submitted for recognition as an American National Standard

SAE J1661

Issued 1993-06-02

PROCEDURE FOR RETROFITTING CFC-12 (R12) MOBILE AIR CONDITIONING SYSTEMS TO HFC-134a (R134a)

1. Scope—The purpose of this SAE Recommended Practice is to provide a service procedure for retrofitting a CFC-12 (R12) system to HFC-134a (R134a) while preserving performance and integrity of the air conditioning system. The steps outlined in this procedure are complete when combined with good service practices and the vehicle manufacturer's recommendations (if available) for retrofitting their models.

Separate service equipment, for R12 and R134a, including refrigerant recovery/recycle, service manifolds, vacuum pumps, and charging equipment shall be used to preserve the purity of the refrigerants and the mobile air conditioning systems. This procedure will minimize release of refrigerant to the atmosphere, and will preserve the integrity of the recycled R12 and R134a supplies.

This document applies to air conditioning systems used to cool the passenger compartment of automobiles, light trucks, and other vehicles with similar R12 systems. Due to technical advancements in recent years, this procedure is recommended for common vehicle platforms produced in the mid-1980s and later. Vehicles produced before this time period may require additional retrofit requirements. Air conditioning systems used on mobile vehicles for refrigerated cargo that have hermetically sealed systems are not covered by this document.

This document is complete only when combined with the requirements of SAE J1657.

2. References

2.1 Applicable Documents—The following publications form a part of this specification to the extent specified herein. The latest issue of SAE publications shall apply.

2.1.1 SAE PUBLICATIONS—Available from SAE, 400 Commonwealth Drive, Warrendale, PA 15096-0001.

SAE J639—Safety and Containment of Refrigerant for Mechanical Vapor Compression Systems Used for Mobile Air Conditioning Systems
SAE J1628—Technical Procedure for Using Electronic Refrigerant Leak Detectors for Service of Mobile Air Conditioning Systems
SAE J1629—Cautionary Statement for Handling HFC-134a During Mobile Air Conditioning Service
SAE J1657—Selection Criteria for Retrofit Refrigerants to Replace CFC-12 (R12) in Mobile Air Conditioning Systems
SAE J1660—Fittings and Labels for Retrofit of CFC-12 (R12) Mobile Air Conditioning Systems to R-134a
SAE J1989—Recommended Service Procedure for the Containment of R-12
SAE J1990—Extraction and Recycle Equipment for Mobile Air Conditioning Systems (R-12)
SAE J1991—Standard of Purity for Use in Mobile Air Conditioning Systems (R-12)
SAE J2064—R-134a Automotive Air Conditioning Hose

SAE Technical Standards Board Rules provide that: "This report is published by SAE to advance the state of technical and engineering sciences. The use of this report is entirely voluntary, and its applicability and suitability for any particular use, including any patent infringement arising therefrom, is the sole responsibility of the user."

SAE reviews each technical report at least every five years at which time it may be reaffirmed, revised, or cancelled. SAE invites your written comments and suggestions.

Copyright 1993 Society of Automotive Engineers, Inc
All rights reserved.

SAE J1661 Issued JUN93

SAE J2099—Standard of Purity for Recycled HFC-134a for Use in Mobile Air Conditioning Systems
SAE J2196—Service Hoses for Automotive Air Conditioning
SAE J2197—HFC-134a Service Hose Fittings for Automotive Air Conditioning Service Equipment
SAE J2209—CFC-12 Extraction Equipment for Mobile Air Conditioning Systems
SAE J2210—HFC-134a Recycling Equipment for Mobile Air Conditioning Systems
SAE J2211—Recommended Service Practice for the Containment of HFC-134a

3. Air Conditioning System Preparation Prior to Retrofit

3.1 Determine that the vehicle air conditioning system has not been previously retrofitted. Talk to the customer and obtain the service history of the air conditioning system.

3.1.1 Check the engine compartment area for a system label to determine the existing system identification and/or if a retrofit label has been installed.

3.1.2 Determine that R12 service ports are on the air conditioning system. R12 high and low side ports. (SAE 3/8 in-24 and 7/16 in-20 refrigeration flares as defined in SAE J639)

3.1.3 Check all service ports and identify the usage (e.g., switches). Refer to 5.3 for retrofit fitting and label requirements.

3.2 Determine possible refrigerant leaks and system performance.

3.2.1 Connect the R-12 manifold set including service hoses that meet SAE J2196 to the system. During initial inspection and service, use R-12 refrigerant recovery/recycle (R12 R/R) equipment meeting SAE J1990 or J2209.

3.2.2 With the engine off, check the air conditioning system pressure. If the system does not have pressure, inspect the system for possible leak points. Follow SAE J1628 Leak Check procedure by adding refrigerant R12 to determine if the system has any leaks. System components that are found to be leaking shall be repaired or replaced in a manner compatible with the retrofit.

3.2.3 With the refrigerant system properly charged, operate the air conditioning system and observe the high and low pressures, panel outlet discharge temperature, and other parameters recommended by the vehicle manufacturer.

3.2.4 Determine necessary repairs and component replacements in addition to those required for retrofitting the vehicle air conditioning system. Refer to 5.2.1 for repairs.

3.3 Using R12 refrigerant recovery/recycle equipment (R12 R/R equipment) meeting SAE J1990 or J2209, recover the refrigerant according to the service procedure in SAE J1989. During refrigerant recovery, observe air conditioning system components (e.g., accumulator) for frosting. If frosting has occurred or if the low side pressure rises above atmospheric pressure within 2 min, additional refrigerant is in the system and it shall be removed. Gently applying heat to the frosted components will reduce the time for the refrigerant recovery process.

3.3.1 To assure recovery of R12 refrigerant during system processing as defined in 3.3 or after flushing as defined in 4.4, the SAE J1989 procedure shall be used. SAE J1989 states, "Start the recovery process and remove the refrigerant from the vehicle air conditioning system. Operate the recovery unit until the vehicle system has been reduced from a pressure to a vacuum. With the recovery unit shut off for at least 5 min, determine that there is no refrigerant remaining in the vehicle air conditioning system. If the vehicle system has pressure, additional recovery operation is required to remove the remaining refrigerant. Repeat the operation until the vehicle air conditioning system vacuum level remains stable for 2 min."

SAE J1661 Issued JUN93

3.4 Evaluate the retrofit requirements which will vary by vehicle and model year.

3.4.1 Improper retrofit procedures may affect performance or result in damage to the air conditioning system. Carefully read the vehicle manufacturer's requirements for retrofitting the particular vehicle air conditioning system to R134a.

3.4.2 Determine the suitable lubricant type to be used with the R134a retrofit refrigerant. Refer to the manufacturer's procedure to determine which components need inspection, cleaning, or replacement. Affected components may include hoses, seals, expansion devices, accumulators, receiver driers, and possibly other components depending on system design.

4. *System Cleanup Procedure*

4.1 R12 Removal—To protect the integrity of the R134a recycled refrigerant supply, R12 must be removed from the air conditioning system before charging with R134a at the end of the retrofit procedure. Service procedures shall reduce the R12 content in the retrofitted system. Excess R12 levels may cause system chemical contamination and system damage. Procedures in 3.3.1 and/or 4.3 and 4.4, when followed, will provide proper R134a purity. Consult the vehicle manufacturer's requirements.

The importance of evacuation per 6.3 in removing R12 must be emphasized. SAE and industry conducted a survey on residual R12 levels in refrigerants sampled from retrofitted air conditioning systems. System cleanup procedures were reviewed to determine their effect on R12 levels. System evacuation after completing the retrofit procedure is the most effective procedure in achieving low R12 levels.

4.2 Lubricant Removal—Depending on the retrofit lubricant choice and the particular air conditioning system, part or all of the mineral oil may need to be removed. Draining oil from components, replacing components, or flushing can be used for this purpose. It is essential to follow the manufacturer's recommendations for removing and replacing lubricant (see 5.2.2).

4.3 Vehicle Manufacturer's Recommended Cleanup Procedure (Procedure 1)

4.3.1 Consult vehicle manufacturer's recommendations, if available. The vehicle manufacturer's recommended service procedures shall meet the R134a purity level, of less than 2.0% R12 in 4.1. These procedures will likely emphasize evacuation for a period of time not less than called for in 6.3.

4.4 Flush the Air Conditioning System With R12 (Procedure 2)

4.4.1 Connect the flushing equipment. Prepare for flushing by opening the air conditioning system to provide a flushing inlet and an outlet to the air conditioning system or component. Consult the vehicle manufacturer's recommended procedure to determine the flushing connections and which components to leave in during the flushing procedure. Check all connections to be sure they are leak-free. For systems which have an air conditioning compressor that is designed to retain oil in the crankcase, consult the manufacturer's procedures to drain oil from the compressor.

4.4.2 Evacuate the portion or component of the air conditioning system and flushing equipment which was open to the atmosphere while making the flushing connections. This will prevent air from being introduced into the R12 flushing equipment.

4.4.3 Flush for the recommended time. Use flushing equipment which separates oil from the R12 flushing medium before returning it to the R12 storage container. At the end of the flushing procedure, the refrigerant in the R12 container shall be recycled to SAE J1991 purity before beginning the next flushing operation.

SAE J1661 Issued JUN93

4.4.4 Completely recover the R12 refrigerant used to flush the air conditioning system or components per SAE J1989 as defined in 3.3.1. Since the air conditioning system or component will be completely filled with liquid R12, the recovery process shall be monitored for frosting of components to assure that all the refrigerant has been removed. Gently apply heat to components which have become frosted during the recovery process. The quantity of oil removed provides an indication of successful flushing.

5. Retrofit to R134a Procedure

5.1 Remove all the R12 service equipment. Disconnect the R12 manifold and R12 R/R equipment from the system. Evacuation and charging will be accomplished with R134a service equipment using fittings per SAE J2197.

5.2 Repair and Retrofit System

5.2.1 If required, repair or replace the necessary system parts. Fix any problems noted in 3.2.4 to assure proper system operation as defined in 6.6.

5.2.2 Charge lubricant type in the amount, location, and manner recommended by the vehicle manufacturer. If the air conditioning system has been flushed, lubricant shall be charged directly into the compressor or the low side near the compressor to provide lubricant to the compressor at first start-up.

5.2.3 Retrofit and reassemble the air conditioning system using the recommended procedures and OEM or equivalent components in 3.4.

5.3 Change service ports and apply labels as defined in SAE J1660. Use only fittings and labels meeting SAE J1660 installed in the manner prescribed in SAE J1660.

6. R-134a Evacuation and Charging Procedure

6.1 Cautionary Statements

6.1.1 CAUTION—Avoid breathing air conditioning refrigerant and lubricant vapor or mist. Exposure may irritate eyes, nose, and throat. To remove HFC-134a from the air conditioning system, use service equipment certified to meet the requirements of SAE J2210 (HFC-134a recycling equipment). Additional health and safety information may be obtained from refrigerant and lubricant manufacturers.

6.1.2 CAUTION—Do not pressure test or leak test HFC-134a service equipment and/or vehicle air conditioning systems with compressed air. Some mixtures of air and HFC-134a have been shown to be combustible at elevated pressures. These mixtures, if ignited, may cause injury or property damage. Additional health and safety information may be obtained from refrigerant manufacturers.

6.1.3 CAUTION—Lubricants used with HFC-134a refrigerant for mobile air conditioning systems may damage the appearance of painted surfaces and plastic parts.

6.2 Connect hoses from the manifold gauge set or the R134a charging equipment to the air conditioning system service ports.

6.3 **Evacuation**—Using an R134a vacuum pump, having fittings defined in SAE J2197, evacuate the air conditioning system for a minimum of 30 min to remove air and trace R12 from the system. Vehicles equipped with front and rear evaporators evacuate the system for at least 45 min. The vacuum pump shall be capable of a vacuum level of 2.7 kPa (29.2 in of mercury below atmospheric adjusted to altitude). The vacuum pump may be part of the R134a service equipment. System manufacturers may recommend longer evacuation time for specific systems.

SAE J1661 Issued JUN93

6.4 With the vacuum pump isolated from the system, check for loss of vacuum as an indication of a system leak. If loss of vacuum occurs, determine if the leak source can be identified and repaired. Repair the leak and evacuate the system for 15 min.

6.5 Charge the air conditioning system with R134a in the amount and manner recommended by the system manufacturer. Be sure that the lubricant has been installed as defined in 5.2.2.

6.6 Operate the air conditioning system to assure that the system is properly operating.

6.6.1 Shut the vehicle off and remove all the service equipment and replace the caps and secondary seals on all service ports.

6.7 Perform a final leak check as defined in SAE J1628 to assure that the system is leak-free.

PREPARED BY THE SAE INTERIOR CLIMATE CONTROL STANDARDS COMMITTEE

SAE The Engineering Society
For Advancing Mobility
Land Sea Air and Space®

400 COMMONWEALTH DRIVE, WARRENDALE, PA 15096

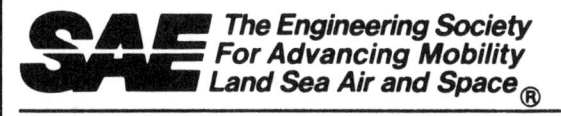

HIGHWAY VEHICLE RECOMMENDED PRACTICE

SAE J1989

Issued October 1989

Submitted for recognition as an American National Standard

RECOMMENDED SERVICE PROCEDURE FOR THE CONTAINMENT OF R-12

1. SCOPE:

   During service of mobile air-conditioning systems, containment of the refrigerant is important. This procedure provides service guidelines for technicians when repairing vehicles and operating equipment defined in SAE J1990.

2. REFERENCES:

   SAE J1990, Extraction and Recycle Equipment for Mobile Automotive Air-Conditioning Systems

3. REFRIGERANT RECOVERY PROCEDURE:

3.1 Connect the recovery unit service hoses, which shall have shutoff valves within 12 in (30 cm) of the service ends, to the vehicle air-conditioning system service ports.

3.2 Operate the recovery equipment as covered by the equipment manufacturers recommended procedure.

3.2.1 Start the recovery process and remove the refrigerant from the vehicle AC system. Operate the recovery unit until the vehicle system has been reduced from a pressure to a vacuum. With the recovery unit shut off for at least 5 min, determine that there is no refrigerant remaining in the vehicle AC system. If the vehicle system has pressure, additional recovery operation is required to remove the remaining refrigerant. Repeat the operation until the vehicle AC system vacuum level remains stable for 2 min.

3.3 Close the valves in the service lines and then remove the service lines from the vehicle system. Proceed with the repair/service. If the recovery equipment has automatic closing valves, be sure they are properly operating.

SAE Technical Board Rules provide that: "This report is published by SAE to advance the state of technical and engineering sciences. The use of this report is entirely voluntary, and its applicability and suitability for any particular use, including any patent infringement arising therefrom, is the sole responsibility of the user."

SAE reviews each technical report at least every five years at which time it may be reaffirmed, revised, or cancelled. SAE invites your written comments and suggestions.

Copyright 1989 Society of Automotive Engineers, Inc.
All rights reserved.

| | J1989 | | | SAE |

4. SERVICE WITH MANIFOLD GAGE SET:

4.1 Service hoses must have shutoff valves in the high, low, and center service hoses within 12 in (30 cm) of the service ends. Valves must be closed prior to hose removal from the air-conditioning system. This will reduce the volume of refrigerant contained in the service hose that would otherwise be vented to atmosphere.

4.2 During all service operations, the valves should be closed until connected to the vehicle air-conditioning system or the charging source to avoid introduction of air and to contain the refrigerant rather than vent open to atmosphere.

4.3 When the manifold gage set is disconnected from the air-conditioning system or when the center hose is moved to another device which cannot accept refrigerant pressure, the gage set hoses should first be attached to the reclaim equipment to recover the refrigerant from the hoses.

5. RECYCLED REFRIGERANT CHECKING PROCEDURE FOR STORED PORTABLE AUXILIARY CONTAINER:

5.1 To determine if the recycled refrigerant container has excess noncondensable gases (air), the container must be stored at a temperature of 65°F (18.3°C) or above for a period of time, 12 h, protected from direct sun.

5.2 Install a calibrated pressure gage, with 1 psig divisions (0.07 kg), to the container and determine the container pressure.

5.3 With a calibrated thermometer, measure the air temperature within 4 in (10 cm) of the container surface.

5.4 Compare the observed container pressure and air temperature to determine if the container exceeds the pressure limits found on Table 1, e.g., air temperature 70°F (21°C) pressure must not exceed 80 psig (5.62 kg/cm^2).

TABLE 1

TEMP°F	PSIG	TEMP°F	PSIG	TEMP°F	PSIG	TEMP°F	PSIG	TEMP°F	PSIG
65	74	75	87	85	102	95	118	105	136
66	75	76	88	86	103	96	120	106	138
67	76	77	90	87	105	97	122	107	140
68	78	78	92	88	107	98	124	108	142
69	79	79	94	89	108	99	125	109	144
70	80	80	96	90	110	100	127	110	146
71	82	81	98	91	111	101	129	111	148
72	83	82	99	92	113	102	130	112	150
73	84	83	100	93	115	103	132	113	152
74	86	84	101	94	116	104	134	114	154

TABLE 1 (Metric)

TEMP°C	PRES	TEMP°C	PRES	TEMP°C	PRES	TEMP°C	PRES	TEMP°C	PRES
18.3	5.20	23.9	6.11	29.4	7.17	35.0	8.29	40.5	9.56
18.8	5.27	24.4	6.18	30.0	7.24	35.5	8.43	41.1	9.70
19.4	5.34	25.0	6.32	30.5	7.38	36.1	8.57	41.6	9.84
20.0	5.48	25.5	6.46	31.1	7.52	36.6	8.71	42.2	9.98
20.5	5.55	26.1	6.60	31.6	7.59	37.2	8.78	42.7	10.12
21.1	5.62	26.6	6.74	32.2	7.73	37.7	8.92	43.3	10.26
21.6	5.76	27.2	6.88	32.7	7.80	38.3	9.06	43.9	10.40
22.2	5.83	27.7	6.95	33.3	7.94	38.8	9.13	44.4	10.54
22.7	5.90	28.3	7.03	33.9	8.08	39.4	9.27	45.0	10.68
23.3	6.04	28.9	7.10	34.4	8.15	40.0	9.42	45.5	10.82

PRES kg/sq cm

5.5 If the container pressure is less than the Table 1 values and has been recycled, limits of noncondensable gases (air) have not been exceeded and the refrigerant may be used.

5.6 If the pressure is greater than the range and the container contains recycled material, slowly vent from the top of the container a small amount of vapor into the recycle equipment until the pressure is less than the pressure shown on Table 1.

5.7 If the container still exceeds the pressure shown on Table 1, the entire contents of the container shall be recycled.

6. CONTAINERS FOR STORAGE OF RECYCLED REFRIGERANT:

6.1 Recycled refrigerant should not be salvaged or stored in disposable refrigerant containers. This is the type of container in which virgin refrigerant is sold. Use only DOT CFR Title 49 or UL approved storage containers for recycled refrigerant.

6.2 Any container of recycled refrigerant that has been stored or transferred must be checked prior to use as defined in Section 5.

7. TRANSFER OF RECYCLED REFRIGERANT:

7.1 When external portable containers are used for transfer, the container must be evacuated to at least 27 in of vacuum (75 mm Hg absolute pressure) prior to transfer of the recycled refrigerant. External portable containers must meet DOT and UL standards.

7.2 To prevent on-site overfilling when transferring to external containers, the safe filling level must be controlled by weight and must not exceed 60% of container gross weight rating.

8. **DISPOSAL OF EMPTY/NEAR EMPTY CONTAINERS:**

8.1 Since all the refrigerant may not be removed from disposable refrigerant containers during normal system charging procedures, empty/near empty container contents should be reclaimed prior to disposal of the container.

8.2 Attach the container to the recovery unit and remove the remaining refrigerant. When the container has been reduced from a pressure to a vacuum, the container valve can be closed. The container should be marked empty and is ready for disposal.

	SAE J1991
SAE The Engineering Society For Advancing Mobility Land Sea Air and Space®	**HIGHWAY VEHICLE STANDARD**
400 COMMONWEALTH DRIVE, WARRENDALE, PA 15096	Issued October 1989
Submitted for recognition as an American National Standard	

STANDARD OF PURITY FOR USE IN MOBILE AIR-CONDITIONING SYSTEMS

FOREWORD: Due to the CFC's damaging effect on the ozone layer, recycle of CFC-12 (R-12) used in mobile air-conditioning systems is required to reduce system venting during normal service operations. Establishing recycle specifications for R-12 will assure that system operation with recycled R-12 will provide the same level of performance as new refrigerant.

Extensive field testing with the EPA and the auto industry indicate that reuse of R-12 removed from mobile air-conditioning systems can be considered, if the refrigerant is cleaned to a specific standard. The purpose of this standard is to establish the specific minimum levels of R-12 purity required for recycled R-12 removed from mobile automotive air-conditioning systems.

1. SCOPE:

   This information applies to refrigerant used to service automobiles, light trucks, and other vehicles with similar CFC-12 systems. Systems used on mobile vehicles for refrigerated cargo that have hermetically sealed, rigid pipe are not covered in this document.

2. REFERENCES

   SAE J1989, Recommended Service Procedure for the Containment of R-12

   SAE J1990, Extraction and Recycle Equipment for Mobile Automotive Air-Conditioning Systems

   ARI Standard 700-88

3. PURITY SPECIFICATION:

   The refrigerant in this document shall have been directly removed from, and intended to be returned to, a mobile air-conditioning system. The contaminants in this recycled refrigerant 12 shall be limited to moisture, refrigerant oil, and noncondensable gases, which shall not exceed the following level:

SAE Technical Board Rules provide that: "This report is published by SAE to advance the state of technical and engineering sciences. The use of this report is entirely voluntary, and its applicability and suitability for any particular use, including any patent infringement arising therefrom, is the sole responsibility of the user."

SAE reviews each technical report at least every five years at which time it may be reaffirmed, revised, or cancelled. SAE invites your written comments and suggestions.

Copyright 1989 Society of Automotive Engineers, Inc.
All rights reserved.

J1991	SAE

3.1 <u>Moisture</u>: 15 ppm by weight.

3.2 <u>Refrigerant Oil</u>: 4000 ppm by weight.

3.3 <u>Noncondensable Gases (Air)</u>: 330 ppm by weight.

4. <u>REFRIGERATION RECYCLE EQUIPMENT USED IN DIRECT MOBILE AIR-CONDITIONING SERVICE OPERATIONS REQUIREMENT</u>:

4.1 The equipment shall meet SAE J1990, which covers additional moisture, acid, and filter requirements.

4.2 The equipment shall have a label indicating that it is certified to meet this document.

5. <u>PURITY SPECIFICATION OF RECYCLED R-12 REFRIGERANT SUPPLIED IN CONTAINERS FROM OTHER RECYCLE SOURCES</u>:

Purity specification of recycled R-12 refrigerant supplied in containers from other recycle sources, for service of mobile air-conditioning systems, shall meet ARI Standard 700-88 (Air Conditioning and Refrigeration Institute).

6. <u>OPERATION OF THE RECYCLE EQUIPMENT</u>:

This shall be done in accordance with SAE J1989.

SAE The Engineering Society For Advancing Mobility Land Sea Air and Space
INTERNATIONAL
400 Commonwealth Drive, Warrendale, PA 15096-0001

SURFACE VEHICLE STANDARD

SAE J2099

Issued 1991-12

Submitted for recognition as an American National Standard

STANDARD OF PURITY FOR RECYCLED HFC-134a FOR USE IN MOBILE AIR-CONDITIONING SYSTEMS

Foreword—The purpose of this SAE Standard is to establish the minimum level of purity required for recycled HFC-134a removed from, and intended for reuse in, mobile air-conditioning systems.

1. *Scope*—This SAE Standard applies to HFC-134a refrigerant used to service motor vehicle passenger compartment air-conditioning systems designed or retrofitted to use HFC-134a. Hermetically sealed, refrigerated cargo systems are not covered by this document.

2. *References*

2.1 **Applicable Documents**—The following publications form a part of this specification to the extent specified herein. The latest issue of SAE publications shall apply.

2.1.1 SAE PUBLICATIONS—Available from SAE, 400 Commonwealth Drive, Warrendale, PA 15096-0001.
SAE J2210—HFC-134a Recycling Equipment for Mobile Air-Conditioning Systems
SAE J2211—Recommended Service Procedure for the Containment of HFC-134a

3. *Purity Specification*—The refrigerant referred to in this document shall have been directly removed from, and intended to be returned to, a mobile air-conditioning system. Contaminants in this recycled refrigerant shall be limited to moisture, refrigerant system lubricant, and noncondensable gases, which, when measured in the refrigerant liquid phase, shall not exceed the following levels:

3.1 **Moisture**—50 ppm by weight

3.2 **Lubricant**—500 ppm by weight

3.3 **Noncondensable Gases (Air)**—150 ppm by weight

4. *Requirements for Recycle Equipment Used in Direct Mobile Air-Conditioning Service Operations*

4.1 Such equipment shall meet J2210, which covers additional moisture, acid, and filter requirements.

5. *Purity of HFC-134a Supplied From Other Sources*—The purity of HFC-134a refrigerant supplied in containers from other sources shall, for servicing mobile air-conditioning systems, meet the refrigerant manufacturers specification for new HFC-134a intended for mobile air-conditioning system use.

6. *Operation of the Recycle Equipment*—Recycle equipment operation shall be in accord with SAE J2211.

PREPARED BY THE SAE INTERIOR CLIMATE CONTROL STANDARDS COMMITTEE

SAE Technical Standards Board Rules provide that: "This report is published by SAE to advance the state of technical and engineering sciences. The use of this report is entirely voluntary, and its applicability and suitability for any particular use, including any patent infringement arising therefrom, is the sole responsibility of the user."

SAE reviews each technical report at least every five years at which time it may be reaffirmed, revised, or cancelled. SAE invites your written comments and suggestions.

Copyright 1991 Society of Automotive Engineers, Inc.
All rights reserved.

SAE J2196

SURFACE VEHICLE STANDARD

Issued 1992-06-02

Submitted for recognition as an American National Standard

SERVICE HOSE FOR AUTOMOTIVE AIR CONDITIONING

1. Scope—This SAE Standard covers reinforced rubber, reinforced thermoplastic, or otherwise constructed hose, or hose assemblies, intended for conducting liquid and gaseous refrigerants for service connections from mobile air-conditioning systems to service equipment such as a manifold gauge set and vacuum pumps or for use internally, in charging stations or service equipment intended for use in servicing mobile air-conditioning systems.

1.1 The hose shall be designed to minimize permeation of refrigerants and contamination of refrigerant passing there through and to be serviceable over a temperature range of −30 to 95 °C. Hose working pressure shall be at least 3.4 MPa and the minimum burst pressure shall be at least 5 times.

2. References

2.1 Applicable Documents

2.1.1 SAE PUBLICATIONS—Available from SAE, 400 Commonwealth Drive, Warrendale, PA 15096-0001.

SAE J51—Automotive Air-Conditioning Hose

SAE J513—Refrigerant Flare Fittings

SAE J639—Safety Practices for Mechanical Vapor Compression Refrigeration Equipment or System used to Cool Passenger Compartments of Motor Vehicles

SAE J2197—Service Hose Fittings

SAE J2210—HFC-134a Recycling Equipment for Mobile Air-Conditioning Systems

2.1.2 ARI PUBLICATIONS—Available from Air Conditioning and Refrigeration Institute, 1501 Wilson Boulevard, Sixth Floor, Arlington, VA 22209.

ARI 720—Refrigerant Access Valves and Hose Connectors

2.1.3 ASTM PUBLICATIONS—Available from ASTM, 1916 Race Street, Philadelphia, PA 19103.

ASTM D 380—Methods of Testing Rubber Hoses

2.2 Definitions

2.2.1 HIGH SIDE SERVICE HOSE is a hose connected between the vehicle high side service port and the manifold gauge set or equipment. For CFC-12 (R-12), it includes a 1/4 female refrigeration flare (FFL) nut on both ends and a shutoff device within 30 cm of the end connected to the serviced system or equipment. For HFC-134a (R-134a), it includes a high side coupling, as defined in SAE J639 and a shutoff device within 30 cm of the connection to the serviced system or equipment, and a 1/2 ACME female nut on the other end.

2.2.2 LOW SIDE SERVICE HOSE is a hose connected between the vehicle low side service port and the gauge manifold, or equipment. For R-12, it includes a 1/4 female refrigeration flare (FFL) nut on both ends and a shutoff device within 30 cm of the end connected to the serviced system or equipment. For R-134a, it includes a low side coupling, as defined in SAE J639, and a shutoff device within 30 cm of the connection to the serviced system or equipment, and a 1/2 ACME female nut on the other end.

2.2.3 UTILITY HOSE is a hose connected between the manifold gauge set and the service equipment (vacuum pump, charging equipment, recovery/recycling unit). For R-12, it includes a 1/4 FFL nut on both ends and a shutoff device within 30 cm of the end connected to the serviced system or equipment. For R-134a, it includes a 1/2 ACME female nut on both ends and a shutoff device within 30 cm of the connection to the serviced system or equipment.

2.2.4 INTERNAL HOSE is a hose connected between components within or as part of service equipment. If the connection is made external to the unit, it shall be a wrench tight connection different than those described in high side service hose, low side service hose and utility hose as previously defined.

2.2.5 CHARGE COUPLING, USED WITH R-134A, is the female connector intended to be used with the vehicle service fittings (ports) as identified in SAE J639.

2.2.6 THE 1/2 ACME FEMALE NUT was established for connecting service hoses to R-134a refrigerant containers to prevent cross contamination of refrigerants. After consideration of existing fittings for refrigerant containers along with manufacturing and safety concerns it was determined that possible cross threading of metric threads could occur. Establishment of the 1/2 ACME thread reduces the chance of cross threading service hoses resulting in leakage and safety concerns.

3. Hose Assembly Construction

3.1 R-12 Hose

3.1.1 No color, fitting restrictions, or shutoff device requirements shall apply to internal hoses. Hoses which use internal or external wrench tight connections shall be exempt from fitting requirements pertaining to the end of the hose so connected.

3.1.2 High side service hoses, low side service hoses, and utility hoses shall be constructed with 1/4 FFL nuts on both ends and shall have a shutoff device within 30 cm of one end of the hose.

3.1.3 A valve core depressor shall be provided on the same end of the hose as the shutoff device. In most cases, valve core pins on the male fittings are located per ARI Standard 720 refrigerant access valves and hose connectors, but other locations have been used.

3.1.4 Adapters will be used to account for different high side vehicle service fittings per SAE J639.

3.1.5 Colors for various hoses shall be:

3.1.5.1 *Low Side Service Hose*—Solid blue is preferred with optional black with continuous blue stripe.

3.1.5.2 *High Side Service Hose*—Solid red is preferred with optional black with continuous red stripe.

3.1.5.3 *Utility Hose*—Solid yellow or solid white is preferred with optional black with yellow or white continuous stripe.

3.1.5.4 Additional marking as noted in Section 5.

3.2 R-134a Hose

3.2.1 No color, fitting restrictions, or shutoff device requirements shall apply to internal hoses. Hoses which use internal or external wrench tight connection shall be exempt from fitting requirements pertaining to the end of the hose so connected.

3.2.2 High side service hose and low side service hose shall be constructed with the charge coupling on one end, a 1/2 ACME female nut per SAE J2197 on the other end, and a shutoff device within 30 cm of the charge coupling end. Charge couplings for high and low side shall meet the requirements and be compatible as defined in SAE J639.

SAE J2196 Issued JUN92

3.2.2.1 Hoses shall be constructed with the charge coupling integral. As defined in SAE J2197, a 14 mm threaded connection for service replacement of the hose portion is optional. The replacement hose shall meet all the other requirements (no charge coupling) of this document.

3.2.3 Utility hose shall have 1/2 ACME female nut per SAE J2197 on both ends and a shutoff device within 30 cm of one end. The end with the shutoff device shall also include a valve core depressor compatible with SAE J2197.

3.2.4 Colors for various hoses shall be:

3.2.4.1 *Low Side Service Hose*—Solid blue with black stripe.

3.2.4.2 *High Side Service Hose*—Solid red with black stripe.

3.2.4.3 *Utility Hose*—Solid yellow with black stripe.

3.2.4.4 See Figure 1 for stripe and marking detail.

3.2.4.5 Additional marking as noted in Section 5.

4. Hose Manufacturer

4.1 Standard sizes are shown in Table 1. In general, the nominal size is determined by the refrigeration fitting rather than the hose I.D.

TABLE 1—STANDARD HOSE SIZES

Nominal Size	Hose I.D. (min) Reference
1/4 inch	4.4 mm
3/8 inch	8.0 mm
1/2 inch	11.1 mm

5. Hose Identification

5.1 The hose shall be identified with "SAE J2196" marking. For R-134a refrigerants "SAE J2196 R-134a" marking is required.

5.2 On R-134a hoses, the refrigerant designation is associated with the stripe and identified in Figure 1.

5.3 Manufacturer's and assembler identification shall be located on the external surface of the hose 180 degrees from the refrigerant marking as identified in Figure 1.

5.4 The external hose identification should be durable for the life of the hose.

5.4.1 The printed information and stripe as required shall be 3 mm minimum in height, and shall be repeated, not to exceed a distance of 30 cm between start and end of the identification.

6. Testing
—The test procedure described in the current ASTM D 380, shall be followed whenever applicable.

6.1 Test Conditions

6.1.1 The temperature of the testing chamber shall be maintained at 23 °C ± 2 °C.

6.2 Refrigerant Containment

6.2.1 Test hose assemblies shall not permit refrigerant loss of marked refrigerant (R-12, R-134a) at a rate greater than 9.8 kg/m^2/year (2.0 lbs/ft^2 year) when tested at 49 °C ± 2 °C.

6.2.2 The containment test is designed to measure, by loss of mass, the rate of refrigerant loss.

SAE J2196 Issued JUN92

HFC-134a

PRINTING & STRIPE 3mm MINIMUM

REPEAT I.D. SPACING 30cm MAXIMUM

MANUFACTURER
ASSEMBLER
INFORMATION

180 DEGREE

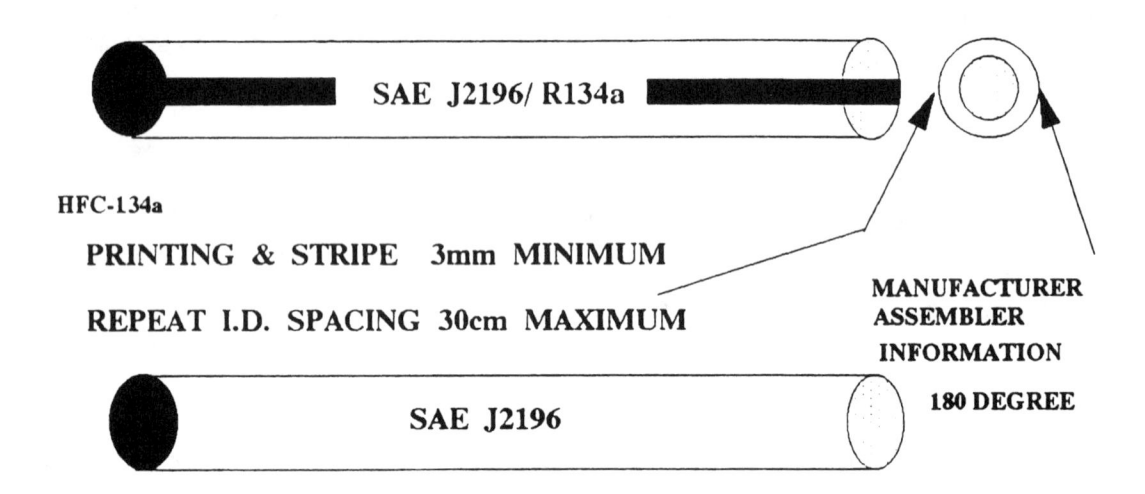

FIGURE 1—SERVICE HOSE

6.2.3 The apparatus required consists of canisters with internal volumes of 475 to 1000 cm^3 and a 21 MPa minimum burst pressure with appropriate fittings to connect to the hose assemblies, halogen detector, circulating air oven capable of maintaining uniform test temperature throughout the test periods, and a weight scale capable of mass measurements to 0.1 g accuracy.

6.2.4 TEST SAMPLE PREPARATION

6.2.4.1 Four hose assemblies, having a free hose length of 1 m, are to be tested.

6.2.4.2 Three of the hose assemblies shall be used for determining the loss of refrigerant and the fourth assembly shall be run as an empty plugged blank to be used as the reference for determining the mass loss of the other hoses.

6.2.4.3 Measure the free length of hose in each assembly at zero gauge pressure to the nearest 1 mm. Connect each of the four hose assemblies to a canister and obtain the total mass of each test unit including end plugs to the nearest 0.1 g.

6.2.4.4 Load three of the test hose assemblies with 0.6 g of liquid refrigerant per cm^3 of each test hose volume to a total variance of ±5 g.

6.2.4.5 Check the loaded test hose assembly with a halogen detector at a sensitivity of 11 g/year to be sure that they do not leak. Any suitable method for safely loading may be used.

6.2.5 TEST PROCEDURE

6.2.5.1 Weigh the test samples and record the mass (weight) of each sample.

6.2.5.2 Place the three loaded and one blank (uncharged) test units in the air oven at the specified temperature (49 °C) for a period of 30 min ± 5 min drive off moisture.

6.2.5.2.1 Do not bend the test sample hose in a curve with a diameter smaller than 20 times the outside diameter of the hose while in the oven.

6.2.5.3 Remove the loaded test sample units from the oven and weigh.

6.2.5.4 Check the test samples for leakage and weigh all samples not less than 15 min or more than 30 min after removal from the oven.

SAE J2196 Issued JUN92

6.2.5.5 Weigh the samples and compare the mass as recorded in 6.2.5.1 to determine if the test sample have lost the test refrigerant charge.

6.2.5.6 If the samples contain a refrigerant charge use the mass recorded in 6.2.5.5 as the original mass for future weight loss comparison.

6.2.5.7 Place the test samples back in the air oven, within 1 h after completion of 6.2.5.6, at the specified temperature for 24 h.

6.2.5.8 At the end of the 24 h period, remove the test samples, weigh and record the data in the same manner as previously specified, and return the test samples to the oven.

6.2.5.9 If a loss of 20 g or greater occurs, discontinue the test, check for leaks, and repeat the procedure as defined in 6.2.5.2.

6.2.5.10 The first 24 h period is considered the preconditioning period. If the test samples as checked in 6.2.5.9 have not leaked consider this recorded mass as the initial mass value.

6.2.5.11 Return the samples to the oven for 72 h.

6.2.5.12 Remove the samples from the oven and weigh and record the mass in the same manner as previously described.

6.2.5.13 Calculate the 72 h mass loss and determine the effusion rate by subtracting the corresponding mass of the blank from that of the loaded test sample unit. Express the refrigerant loss rate in kg/m^2/year.

6.2.5.14 Calculate the rate of loss of refrigerant mass for the loaded test sample unit as follows:

$$R = K/D * ([(A-B)/L1]-[(C-E)/L2]) \quad \text{(Eq. 1)}$$

where:

A = Initial mass after preconditioning period of loaded test unit, g

B = Final mass after 72 h period of loaded test unit, g.

C = Initial mass after preconditioning period of blank test unit, g.

D = Nominal hose inside diameter, mm.

E = Final mass after 72 h period of blank test unit, g.

K = 38.7

R = Rate of refrigerant mass loss, kilograms per square meter per year.

L1 = Free length of loaded test unit, m.

L2 = Free hose length of blank test unit, m.

6.3 Refrigerant/Oil (Lubricant) Exposure

6.3.1 Three 457 mm long samples of the hose assembly are required for this test. The hose shall remain intact for this test.

6.3.2 The hose shall be filled to 70% capacity with a mixture of 95% refrigerant and 5% refrigerant lubricant.

6.3.2.1 Testing for R-12 hoses shall use SUNISO 5GS oil or equivalent.

6.3.2.2 Testing for R-134a hoses shall use ICI products lubricant (PAG) EMKAROX RL 118 or equivalent.

6.3.3 The hose assemblies containing the refrigerant/lubricant mixture shall be immersed in ASTM Oil No. 3 at 80 °C for 168 h.

6.3.4 Immediately following the exposure test, the test sample shall withstand, without failure, the tensile test of the assembly required in 6.8 and the burst pressure in 6.7.

6.4 Vacuum Test

SAE J2196 Issued JUN92

6.4.1 The test sample hose shall have a free length of 610 mm.

6.4.1.1 The collapse of the hose shall not exceed 20% of the original outside diameter when subjected to reduced pressure (vacuum) of 1000 micrometers of Hg (microns) absolute for 2 min.

6.4.1.2 Bend the test hose assembly to a "U" shape with the inside radius at the base of the "U" being 20 times the nominal size of the hose as identified in Table 1 in 4.1.

6.4.1.3 Apply a reduced pressure (vacuum) of 1000 microns absolute to the bent hose assembly for 2 min. At the end of the 2 min period, while the hose is still under reduced pressure, measure the outside diameter of the hose at the base of the "U" to determine the minimum diameter in any plane.

6.5 Aging Test

6.5.1 The test sample hose shall show no cracks or other disintegration when tested as specified after aging at 95 °C ± 2 °C for 168 h.

6.5.2 The test sample hose, which had been used for vacuum testing in 6.4, shall have a length of 610 mm.

6.5.3 Fill the interior of the hose with nitrogen to atmospheric pressure and cap the open ends.

6.5.4 The hose assembly shall be wrapped around a mandrel (metal tube) having a diameter 20 times the nominal hose size as defined in Chart 1 of 4.1.

6.5.5 Place the test sample in the air circulation oven for the time and temperature defined in 6.5.1.

6.5.6 After removal from the oven, allow the hose assembly to cool to room temperature, then remove it from the mandrel and lay in a straight length and examine the hose for external cracks or other disintegration.

6.5.7 Load the hose with nitrogen to 2.4 MPa.

6.5.8 Place the hose assembly under water.

6.5.8.1 Inspect after 5 min and report any bubbling from the hose assembly as evidence of cracking or disintegration.

6.6 Cold Test

6.6.1 The hose shall show no evidence of cracking or breaking when tested as specified.

6.6.2 The test sample hose shall have a length of 457 mm.

6.6.3 Fill the interior of the hose with the appropriate refrigerant (R-12, R-134a) to 70% of capacity at room temperature (24 °C) and plug the open ends.

6.6.4 Place the test sample in an air circulation oven at 70 °C ± 2 °C for 48 h.

6.6.5 Remove the hose assembly from the oven and allow it to cool to room temperature.

6.6.6 Place the hose assembly in a straight position along with a mandrel (metal tube), having a diameter 20 times the nominal hose size as defined in Chart 1 of 4.1, in a cold chamber at −30 °C ± 2 °C for 24 h.

6.6.7 After 24 h, without removing the test material from the cold chamber, bend the hose through 180 degrees over the mandrel at a uniform rate within a time period of 4 to 8 s.

6.6.8 Remove the hose assembly from the cold chamber and allow to warm to room temperature.

6.6.9 Place the hose assembly under an internal hydrostatic pressure of 2.4 MPa for a 5 min period.

6.6.10 Inspect and report any leakage from the hose assembly as evidence of cracking or disintegration.

SAE J2196 Issued JUN92

6.7 Bursting Strength

6.7.1 The minimum bursting strength for all hose assemblies shall be 17.2 MPa. Perform hydrostatic test per ASTM D 380 using the "Straight Bursting Test Method."

6.8 Tensile Test of Hose Assembly

6.8.1 The minimum force required to pull the hose adapter and separate the hose from the coupling shall not be less than 534 N.

6.8.2 The test hose shall have a minimum free hose length of 300 mm.

6.8.3 The hose assembly shall be mounted to a test apparatus having a crosshead speed not to exceed 25 mm per minute.

PREPARED BY THE SAE INTERIOR CLIMATE CONTROL STANDARDS COMMITTEE

SURFACE VEHICLE STANDARD

SAE J2197

Issued 1992-06-02

Submitted for recognition as an American National Standard

HFC-134a (R-134a) SERVICE HOSE FITTINGS FOR AUTOMOTIVE AIR-CONDITIONING SERVICE EQUIPMENT

Foreword—The purpose of this SAE Standard is to establish specific but unique fittings for service equipment used in maintaining HFC-134a (R-134a) systems. This is necessary to avoid cross mixing of refrigerant and lubricants from CFC based systems. This applies only to systems specifically designed for or retrofitted to R-134a. Hermetically sealed appliances and refrigerated cargo systems are not covered by this document.

1. Scope

1.1 This SAE Standard covers fittings intended for connecting service hoses, per SAE J2196, from Mobile Air-Conditioning Systems to service equipment such as manifold gauges, vacuum pumps and air-conditioning charging, recovery and recycling equipment. (Figure 1)

1.2 Due to similarities between English and metric thread sizes a single, unique ACME thread fitting is specified. This fitting was recommended by the Compressed Gas Association (CGA), Connection Standards Committee Task Force as one which could be qualified to meet their requirements for use and safety in a time frame consistent with the introduction of R-134a. It was selected because its unique design would reduce the likelihood of cross-treading service hoses on R-12/R-134a refrigerant storage containers and service equipment.

1.3 The high and low pressure hose in J2196 requires the charge coupling (used to connect service hoses to vehicle access ports) to be an integral part of the hose assembly. To allow removal of the hose from the coupling for hose replacement only, a two-piece construction with a wrench tight connection is permitted. Specifications covering this fitting are provided.

2. References

2.1 Applicable Documents—The following publications form a part of this specification to the extent specified herein. The latest issue of SAE Publications shall apply.

2.1.1 SAE PUBLICATIONS—Available from SAE, 400 Commonwealth Drive, Warrendale, PA 15096-0001.

SAE J639—Vehicle Service Coupling

SAE J2196—Service Hose for Automotive Air Conditioning

SAE J2210—HFC-134a Recycling Equipment for Mobile Air-Conditioning Systems

2.1.2 ARI PUBLICATIONS—Available from Air Conditioning and Refrigeration Institute, 1501 Wilson Boulevard, Sixth Floor, Arlington, VA 22209.

ARI 720—Refrigerant Access Valves and Hose Connectors

SAE J2197 Issued JUN92

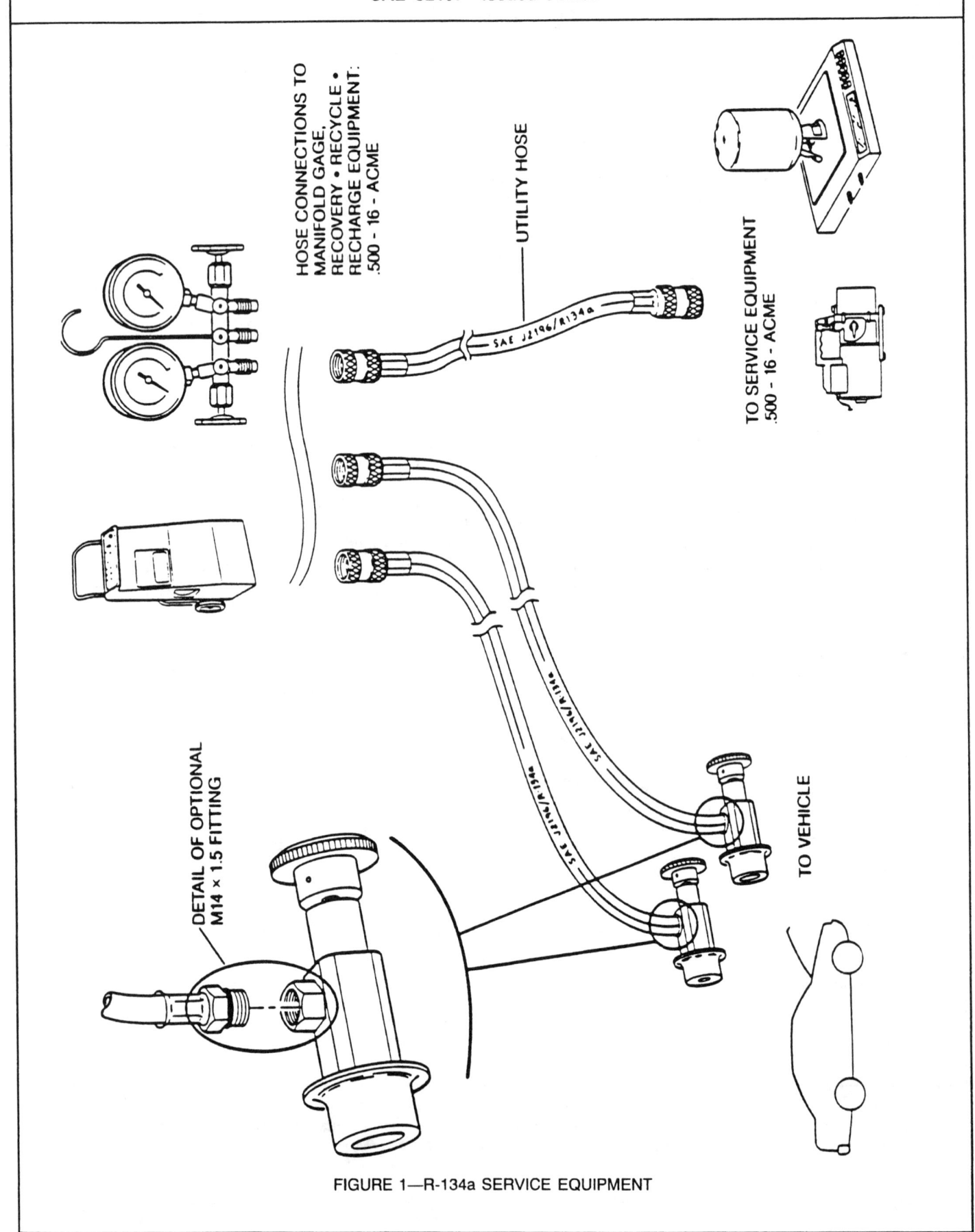

FIGURE 1—R-134a SERVICE EQUIPMENT

SAE J2197 Issued JUN92

3. Specification and Application Description

3.1 0.500 in × 16-2G ACME—Right Hand Thread, Cylinder Valve Outlet Connection—Compressed Gas Association, Inc. Connection No. 167. (Figure 2)

3.1.1 The Connection shall be used on all R-134a refrigerant storage containers liquid and vapor outlet connections. It will also be used for all R-134a service equipment including manifold gauge hose connections, utility hose connection to the vacuum pump, and charging, recovery and recycling equipment as defined in SAE J2210.

3.1.2 Applications which will require the use of valve cores should locate the valve core in accordance with ARI 720.

3.2 M14 × 1.5-6G right hand thread, SAE Hose Barb connection. (Figure 3)

LIMITED STANDARD CYLINDER VALVE OUTLET CONNECTION FOR PRESSURES UP TO 500 PSIG (3450 kPa) FOR TETRAFLUOROETHANE (R-134a) AUTOMOTIVE USE

		VALVE OUTLET
Thread		0.500 -16-ACME-2G-RH-EXT
Major Dia.		0.5000—0.4950 (12.700—12.573)
Pitch Dia.		0.4631—0.4514 (11.762—11.466)
Minor Dia.		0.4275—0.4215 (10.858—10.707)
Bore Dia.	A	0.188 ± 0.002 (4.78 ± 0.05)
Relief Dia.	B	0.360 ± 0.010 (9.14 ± 0.25)
Cut Back	C	0.16 (4.1)
Full Thread	D	0.625 Min. (15.88) Min.

Dimensions are in (mm)

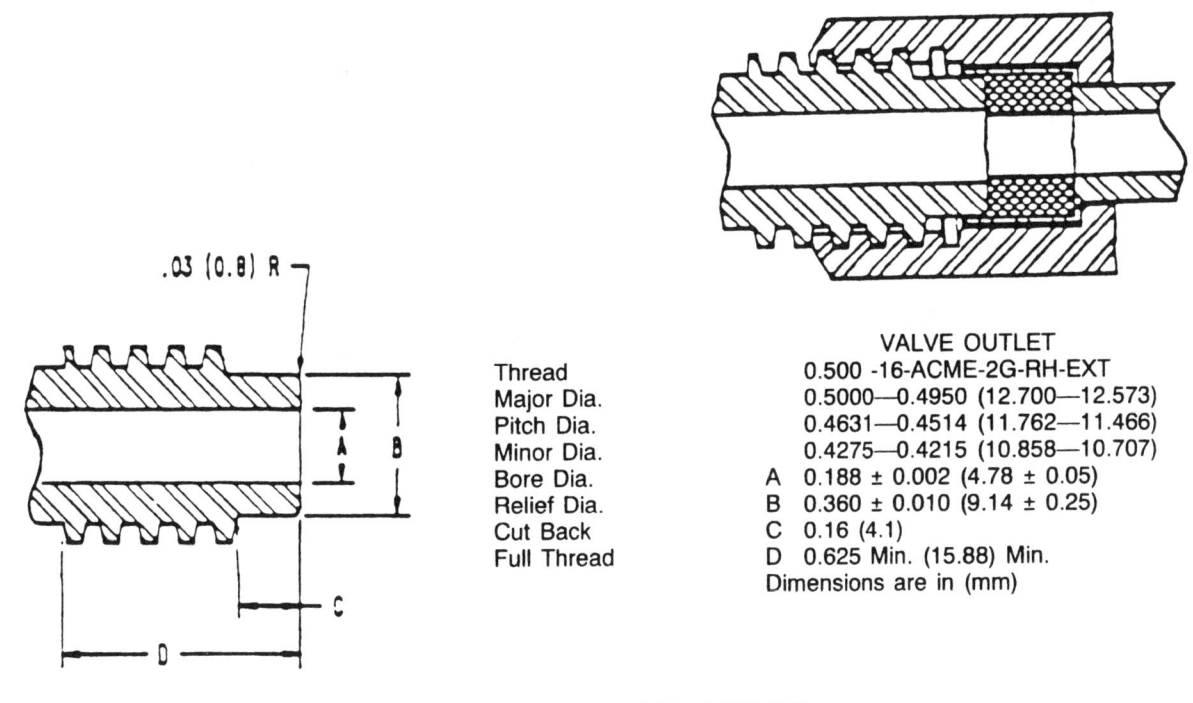

FIGURE 2—0.500 in—16-ACME-2G-RH-EXT

3.2.1 This fitting may be used as an option to a nonserviceable connection of the charge coupling to the service hose assembly and will require a secure, wrench tight connection.

4. Functional Description

4.1 The high pressure hose assembly shall meet SAE J2196 requirements and will be terminated at one end with the 0.500 in × 16—ACME threaded nut. The other end will be permanently attached to the SAE J639 service charge coupling or terminated with the optional M14 × 1.5-6G external thread/male hose barb fitting.

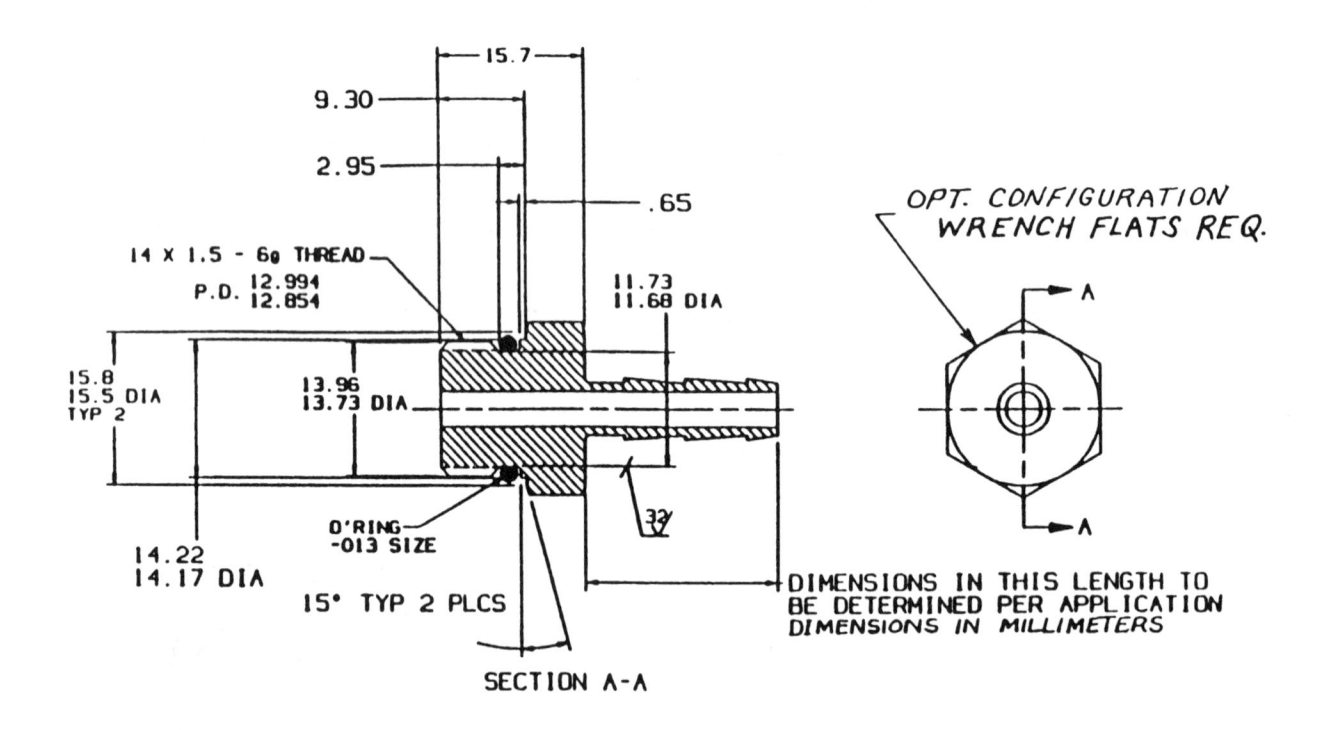

FIGURE 3—SAE HOSE BARB R-134a SERVICE ADAPTER

4.2 The low pressure hose assembly shall meet SAE J2196 requirements and will be terminated at one end with the 0.500 in × 16—ACME threaded nut. The other end will be permanently attached to the SAE J639 service charge coupling or terminated with the optional M14 × 1.5-6G external thread/male hose barb fitting.

4.3 The utility hose shall meet SAE J2196 requirements and will be terminated at both ends using 0.500 in × 16—ACME threaded nut.

4.3.1 Utility hose used on four hose gauge systems should conform to requirements.

4.4 Manifold Gauge Assembly shall require three or four 0.500 in × 16—ACME male threaded connections.

4.5 Containers disposable or refillable shall require 0.500 in × 16—ACME male threaded connections with shut off valves.

4.6 Refrigerant recovery, charging stations and stand-alone vacuum pumps shall require 0.500 in × 16—ACME male threaded connection unless an internal, nonserviceable connection is made by the equipment manufacturer.

4.7 High and low pressure charge couplings shall be constructed with an internal, M14 × 1.5-6H right hand thread connection as an option to attaching the hose assembly with a nonserviceable connection. (Figure 4)

5. Testing—This test procedure is for the qualification of new connection for R-134a automotive air-conditioning system service equipment.

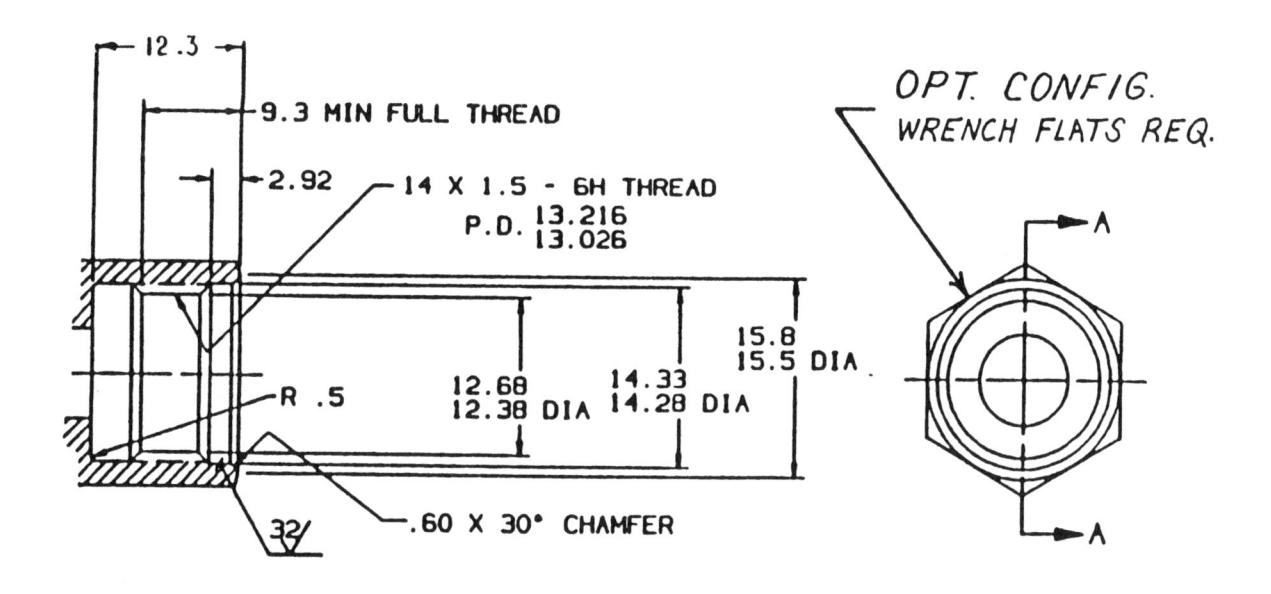

SAE J2197 Issued JUN92

FIGURE 4—SAE SPUD R-134a SERVICE ADAPTER

5.1 Determine the minimum torque necessary for a gas tight shutoff between the nipple and valve body at a gas pressure equal to the maximum rated working pressure per SAE J2196. For cycling purposes, twice this shutoff torque will be used to simulate normally applied field torque.

5.2 Cycling is to be conducted at atmospheric pressure, since that is the pressure at which connections are normally made.

5.3 Before and after cycling, measurements of the connection shall be recorded (such as threaded elements, nipple bore diameters, and any other dimensions that may be subject to change) due to repeated tightenings.

5.4 Each connection is to be cycled 500 times with tightening to the torque determined in 5.1. One cycle consists of tightening to the predetermined torque and then loosening to, at most, finger tight.

5.5 After each 100 cycles, the torque required to achieve gas tight shutoff at test pressure shall be recorded to determine if there is any abnormal torque buildup in shutoff requirements. The measurements indicated in 5.3 shall also be recorded at this interval to determine if there is any abnormal deformation of parts.

5.6 Each connection shall be subjected to a hydrostatic test and must withstand a pressure of a least 4 times the maximum rated working pressure per SAE J2196 without structure failure.

5.7 After completion of the previous tests, the results will be recorded on a suitable test report form which will be kept on file at the Compressed Gas Association office.

5.7.1 Testing of either a left hand or right hand connection of identical design (except for thread direction) automatically qualifies the untested connection of the opposite thread direction. (The direction of the thread does not effect the structural integrity of the design.)

PREPARED BY THE SAE INTERIOR CLIMATE CONTROL STANDARDS COMMITTEE

SAE The Engineering Society For Advancing Mobility Land Sea Air and Space

INTERNATIONAL

400 Commonwealth Drive, Warrendale, PA 15096-0001

SURFACE VEHICLE RECOMMENDED PRACTICE

Submitted for recognition as an American National Standard

SAE J2211

Issued 1991-12

RECOMMENDED SERVICE PROCEDURE FOR THE CONTAINMENT OF HFC-134a

1. Scope—Refrigerant containment is an important part of servicing mobile air-conditioning systems. This procedure provides guidelines for technicians for servicing mobile air-conditioning systems and operating refrigerant recycling equipment designed for HFC-134a (described in SAE J2210).

2. References

2.1 Applicable Documents—The following publications form a part of this specification to the extent specified herein. The latest issue of SAE publications shall apply.

2.1.1 SAE PUBLICATIONS—Available from SAE, 400 Commonwealth Drive, Warrendale, PA 15096-0001.

SAE J2196—Service Hoses for Mobile Air-Conditioning Systems
SAE J2197—Service Hose Fittings for Automotive Air-Conditioning
SAE J2210—Refrigerant Recycling Equipment for HFC-134a Mobile Air-Conditioning Systems
SAE J2219—Concerns to the Mobile Air-Conditioning Industry

2.2 Definitions

2.2.1 RECOVERY/RECYCLING (R/R) UNIT—Refers to a single piece of equipment that performs both functions of recovery and recycling of refrigerants per SAE J2210.

2.2.2 RECOVERY—Refers to that portion of the R/R unit operation that removes the refrigerant from the mobile air-conditioning system and places it in the R/R unit storage container.

2.2.3 RECYCLING—Refers to that portion of the R/R unit operation that processes the refrigerant for reuse on the same job site to the purity specifications of SAE J2099.

3. Service Procedure

3.1 Connect the recycling unit service hoses, which shall have shutoff devices (e.g., valves) within 30 cm (12 in) of the service ends, to the vehicle air-conditioning (A/C) service ports. Hoses shall conform to SAE J2196 and fittings shall conform to SAE J2197.

3.2 Operate the recycling equipment per the equipment manufacturer's recommended procedure.

3.2.1 Verify that the vehicle A/C system has refrigerant pressure. Do not attempt to recycle refrigerant from a discharged system as this will introduce air (noncondensable gas) into the recycling equipment which must later be removed by purging.

3.2.2 Begin the recycling process by removing the refrigerant from the vehicle A/C system. Continue the process until the system pressure has been reduced to a minimum of 102 mm (4 in) of Mercury below atmospheric pressure (vacuum). If A/C components show evidence of icing, the component can be gently heated to facilitate refrigerant removal. With the recycling unit shut off for at least

SAE J2211 Issued DEC91

5 min, check A/C system pressure. If this pressure has risen above vacuum (0 psig), additional recycler operation is required to remove the remaining refrigerant. Repeat the operation until the system pressure remains stable at vacuum for 2 min.

3.3 Close the valves in the service lines and then remove the service lines from the vehicle system. If the recovery equipment has automatic closing valves, be sure they are operating properly. Proceed with the repair/service.

3.4 Upon completion of refrigerant removal from the A/C system, determine the amount of lubricant removed during the process and replenish the system with new lubricant, which is identified on the A/C system label. Used lubricant should be discarded per applicable federal, state, and local requirements.

4. Service with a Manifold Gauge Set

4.1 High-side, low-side, and center service hoses must have shutoff devices (e.g., valves) within 30 cm (12 in) of the service ends. Valves must be closed prior to hose removal from the A/C system to prevent refrigerant loss to the atmosphere.

4.2 During all service operations, service hose valves should be closed until connected to the vehicle A/C system or to the charging source to exclude air and/or contain the refrigerant.

4.3 When the manifold gauge set is disconnected from the A/C system, or when the center hose is moved to another device that cannot accept refrigerant pressure, the gauge set hoses should be attached to the recycling equipment to recover the refrigerant from the hoses.

5. Supplemental Refrigerant Checking Procedure for Stored Portable Containers

5.1 Certified recycling equipment and the accompanying recycling procedure, when properly followed, will deliver use-ready refrigerant. In the event that the full recycling procedure was not followed or the technician is unsure about the noncondensble gas content of a given tank of refrigerant, this procedure can be used to determine whether the recycled refrigerant container meets the specification for noncondensable gases (air).

NOTE: The use of refrigerant with excess air will result in higher system operating pressures and may cause A/C system damage.

5.2 The container must be stored at a temperature of 18.3 °C (65 °F) or above for at least 12 h, protected from direct sunlight.

5.3 Install a calibrated pressure gauge, with 6.9 kPa (1 psig) divisions, on the container and read container pressure.

5.4 With a calibrated thermometer, measure the air temperature within 10 cm (4 in) of the container surface.

5.5 Compare the observed container pressure and air temperature to the values given in Tables 1 and 2 to determine whether the container pressure is below the pressure limit given in the Table. For example, at an air temperature of 21 °C (70 °F), the container pressure must not exceed 524 kPa (76 psig).

5.6 If the refrigerant in the container has been recycled and the container pressure is less than the limit in Tables 1 and 2, the refrigerant may be used.

5.7 If the refrigerant in the container has been recycled and the container pressure exceeds the limit in Tables 1 and 2, slowly vent, from the top of the container, a small amount of vapor into the recycle equipment until the pressure is less than the pressure shown in Tables 1 and 2.

TABLE 1—MAXIMUM ALLOWABLE CONTAINER PRESSURE (METRIC)

Temp, C(F)	kPa	Temp, C(F)	kPa	Temp, C(F)	kPa	Temp, C(F)	kPa
18 (65)	476	26 (79)	621	34 (93)	793	42 (108)	1007
19 (66)	483	27 (81)	642	35 (95)	814	43 (109)	1027
20 (68)	503	28 (82)	655	36 (97)	841	44 (111)	1055
21 (70)	524	29 (84)	676	37 (99)	876	45 (113)	1089
22 (72)	545	30 (86)	703	38 (100)	889	46 (115)	1124
23 (73)	552	31 (88)	724	39 (102)	917	47 (117)	1158
24 (75)	572	32 (90)	752	40 (104)	945	48 (118)	1179
25 (77)	593	33 (91)	765	41 (106)	979	49 (120)	1214

TABLE 2—MAXIMUM ALLOWABLE CONTAINER PRESSURE (ENGLISH)

Temp, F	psig	Temp, F	psig	Temp, F	psig	Temp, F	psig
65	69	79	90	93	115	107	144
66	70	80	91	94	117	108	146
67	71	81	93	95	118	109	149
68	73	82	95	96	120	110	151
69	74	83	96	97	122	111	153
70	76	84	98	98	125	112	156
71	77	85	100	99	127	113	158
72	79	86	102	100	129	114	160
73	80	87	103	101	131	115	163
74	82	88	105	102	133	116	165
75	83	89	107	103	135	117	168
76	85	90	109	104	137	118	171
77	86	91	111	105	139	119	173
78	88	92	113	106	142	120	176

5.8 If, after shaking the container and letting it stand for a few minutes, the container pressure still exceeds the pressure limit shown in Tables 1 and 2, the entire contents of the container shall be recycled.

6. Containers for Storage of Recycled Refrigerant

6.1 Recycled refrigerant should not be salvaged or stored in disposable containers (this is one common type of container in which new refrigerant is sold). Use only DOT CFR Title 49 or UL approved storage containers, specifically marked for HFC-134a, for recycled refrigerant.

6.2 Any container of recycled refrigerant that has been stored or transferred must be checked prior to use as defined in Section 5.

6.3 Evacuate new tanks to at least 635 mm Hg (25 in Hg) below atmospheric pressure (vacuum) prior to first use.

7. Transfer of Recycled Refrigerant

7.1 When external portable containers are used for transfer, the container must be evacuated to at least 635 mm (25 in Hg) below atmospheric pressure (vacuum) prior to transfer of the recycled refrigerant to the container. External portable containers must meet DOT and UL standards.

7.2 To prevent on-site overfilling when transferring to external containers, the safe filling level must be controlled by weight and must not exceed 60% of the container gross weight rating.

8. Safety Note for HFC-134a

8.1 HFC-134a has been shown to be nonflammable at ambient temperature and atmospheric pressure. However, recent tests under controlled conditions have indicated that, at pressures above atmospheric and with air concentrations greater than 60% by volume, HFC-134a can form combustible mixtures. While it is recognized that an ignition source is also required for combustion to occur, the presence of combustible mixtures is a potentially dangerous situation and should be avoided.

8.2 Under NO CIRCUMSTANCE should any equipment be pressure tested or leak tested with air/HFC-134a mixtures. Do not use compressed air (shop air) for leak detection in HFC-134a systems.

9. Disposal of Empty/Near Empty Containers

9.1 Since all refrigerant may not have been removed from disposable refrigerant containers during normal system charging procedures, empty/near empty container contents should be recycled prior to disposal of the container.

9.2 Attach the container to the recycling unit and remove the remaining refrigerant. When the container has been reduced from a pressure to a vacuum, the container valve can be closed and the container can be removed from the unit. The container should be marked "Empty," after which it is ready for disposal.

PREPARED BY THE SAE INTERIOR CLIMATE CONTROL STANDARDS COMMITTEE

SAE *The Engineering Society For Advancing Mobility Land Sea Air and Space*
INTERNATIONAL

400 Commonwealth Drive, Warrendale, PA 15096-0001

SURFACE VEHICLE INFORMATION REPORT

SAE J2219	REV. OCT94
Issued 1991-09 Revised 1994-10	
Superseding J2219 SEP91	

Submitted for recognition as an American National Standard

(R) MOBILE AIR CONDITIONING INDUSTRY CRITERIA AND GUIDELINES

1. Scope—The purpose of this SAE Information Report is to provide information on refrigerant issues of concern to the mobile air-conditioning industry.

2. References

2.1 Applicable Documents—The following publications form a part of this document to the extent specified herein. Specific detail information shall be obtained from the appropriate SAE document. The latest issue of SAE Publications shall apply.

2.1.1 SAE Publications—Available from SAE, 400 Commonwealth Drive, Warrendale, PA 15096-0001.

2.1.1.1 Service Activities

SAE J639—Safety and Containment of Refrigerant for Mechanical Vapor Compression Systems used for Mobile Air Conditioning Systems
SAE J1629—Cautionary Statements for Handling HFC-134a During Mobile Air Conditioning Service
SAE J2196—Service Hose for Automotive Air Conditioning
SAE J2197—HFC-134a Service Hose Fittings for Automotive Air Conditioning Service Equipment

2.1.1.2 Technician Service Procedures

SAE J1628—Technician Procedure for Using Electronic Refrigerant Leak Detectors for Service of Mobile Air Conditioning Systems
SAE J1629—Cautionary Statements For Handling HFC-134a
SAE J1989—Recommended Service Procedure for Containment of R12
SAE J2211—Recommended Service Procedure for Containment of HFC-134a

2.1.1.3 Service Equipment

SAE J1627—Rating Criteria for Electronic Leak Detectors
SAE J1990—Extraction and Recycle Equipment for Mobile Automotive Air Conditioning Systems
SAE J1991—Standard of Purity for use in Mobile Air Conditioning Systems
SAE J2209—CFC-12 Extraction Equipment for Mobile Air Conditioning Systems
SAE J2210—HFC-134a Recycling Equipment for Mobile Air Conditioning Systems
SAE J2099—Standard of Purity for Recycled HFC-134a for use in Mobile Air Conditioning Systems
SAE J1732—HFC-134a Extraction Equipment For Mobile Air Condition Systems
SAE J1770—Automotive Refrigerant Recycle Equipment for Multiple Refrigerants (R12/R134a)
SAE J1771—Refrigerant Identifiers

SAE Technical Standards Board Rules provide that: "This report is published by SAE to advance the state of technical and engineering sciences. The use of this report is entirely voluntary, and its applicability and suitability for any particular use, including any patent infringement arising therefrom, is the sole responsibility of the user."

SAE reviews each technical report at least every five years at which time it may be reaffirmed, revised, or cancelled. SAE invites your written comments and suggestions.

Copyright 1994 Society of Automotive Engineers, Inc.
All rights reserved.

SAE J2219 Revised OCT94

2.1.1.4 System Components

    SAE J51—Automotive Air Conditioning Hose
    SAE J2064—R134a Refrigerant Automotive Air Conditioning Hose

2.1.1.5 Retrofit Documents

    SAE J1657—Selection Criteria for Retrofit Refrigerants to Replace R12 in Mobile Air Conditioning Systems
    SAE J1658—Alternate Refrigerant Consistency Criteria for Use in Mobile Air Conditioning Systems
    SAE J1659—Vehicle Testing Requirements for Replacement Refrigerants for use in R12 Mobile Air Conditioning Systems
    SAE J1660—Fittings and Labels for Retrofit or R12 Mobile Air Conditioning Systems to R134a
    SAE J1661—Procedure for Retrofitting R12 Mobile Air Conditioning Systems to R134a
    SAE J1662—Material Compatibility With Alternate Refrigerants

2.1.2 Other Publications

    1990 Federal Clean Air Act, Section 608 and 609
    ARI Standard 700-93

3. CFC-12 Phase-Out—CFCs have been shown to be detrimental to the Earth's ozone layer which acts to shield the Earth from the sun's harmful ultraviolet rays. In response to this threat, the United Nations was successful in bringing about an international agreement, known as the Montreal Protocol, to phase-out the production of all CFCs. In the United States, the Clean Air Act of 1990, and action by President Bush, supported the Montreal Protocol by calling for an accelerated phase-down that started in 1991 with full production ban on December 31, 1995. It is legal to sell and use CFC-12 for servicing mobile air conditioning systems until supplies are no longer available.

3.1 CFC-12 Shortages Predicted—The phase-down will result in progressively less refrigerant being available for service. This will mean that shortages in the supply of CFC-12 will occur in the 1990s. Vehicle OEMs were fully aware of this situation and worked both to conserve the available supply of CFC-12 and to deal effectively with retrofitting vehicles with R134a refrigerant when appropriate.

3.1.1 The Federal government imposed a tax on the sale of new CFCs. The tax amount has increased each year and new product in inventory, in excess of 400 pounds, is subject to a floor stock tax at the time of each increase.

    NOTE—Recycled refrigerant from mobile air conditioning systems is not taxable.

3.2 Federal Clean Air Act Section 609—Effective July 14, 1992, prohibit the release of CFC-12 and HCFC refrigerants during service of mobile air conditioning systems. Recycle of HFC-134a used in mobile air conditioning systems is required during air conditioning system service effective November 15, 1995.

3.2.1 Some larger road vehicles, such as buses, that use HCFC-22 for cooling systems or refrigerant systems for cargo are not covered under the automotive requirements and must comply with Section 608 Type II technician certification. Speciality vehicles such as off-road and farm equipment that use automotive type air conditioning systems that are identified under Section 608 must follow the service requirements identified under Section 609 to be in compliance.

3.2.2 The intent of SAE "J" standards is to assure that the recycled refrigerant used in servicing mobile air conditioning systems provides a purity that will not affect the performance, operation, and warranty of the system. In SAE J1991 (R12) and J2099 (R134a) purity specifications, the document states "the refrigerant in this document shall have been directly removed from, and intended to be returned to, a mobile air conditioning system." The purity specification of reclaimed R12 or R134a refrigerant supplied in containers from other sources, for service of mobile air-conditioning system, shall meet the appropriate ARI Standard 700 (which is an industry purity standard for refrigerants).

3.2.3 The SAE documents J1989 and J1990 are referred to in Section 609 of the Federal Clean Air Act, and also in many state and local laws.

3.3 Equipment Certification—Certified recycle equipment is required by the Clean Air Act to meet SAE J1990 standard.

3.3.1 Equipment Certification must include a label stating "design certified for compliance with the appropriate SAE J document," (e.g., SAE J1991 (R12) or SAE J2099 (R134a)).

3.3.2 Equipment that has safety certification, such as Underwriters Laboratories "UL," does not mean it is in compliance with SAE requirements. The equipment must also have SAE J1991 certification to comply with the Clean Air Act.

3.4 HFC-134a The New OEM Refrigerant—The auto industry selected HFC-134a, which is non-ozone depleting, for new vehicle production starting with 1992 models. The new HFC-134a system phase-in was completed in 1994.

3.4.1 The OEMs have established the necessary procedures and service information for maintaining these HFC-134a Systems.

3.4.2 SAE documents also cover service, containment, and recycle requirements for HFC-134a systems.

4. Refrigerant Recycling Required—SAE, in conjunction with Environmental Protection Agency (EPA) and the auto industry, developed documents covering servicing procedures of mobile systems. These include service procedures, recycle equipment specifications, and standard of purity for recycled refrigerants.

4.1 Service Equipment

4.1.1 The mobile air conditioning industry has established performance certification requirements for recycle and extraction equipment and purity requirements for recycle equipment. Use of certified ARI-740 equipment cannot be used to service mobile air conditioning systems unless it complies with SAE refrigerant purity requirements, or Section 609 of The Clean Air Act requirements.

4.2 This group of SAE documents address equipment and purity requirements for both R12 and R134a refrigerants.

4.2.1 SAE J1990—EXTRACTION AND RECYCLE EQUIPMENT FOR MOBILE AUTOMOTIVE AIR CONDITIONING SYSTEMS—This covers equipment certification for recycling CFC-12 to meet the standard of purity.

4.2.2 SAE J2209—CFC-12 EXTRACTION EQUIPMENT FOR MOBILE AIR CONDITIONING SYSTEMS—This covers equipment certification for removal of CFC-12 from mobile A/C systems that shall be sent off-site for process to meet the appropriate ARI 700 purity level.

4.2.3 SAE J2210—HFC-134a Recycling Equipment for Mobile Air Conditioning Systems—This covers equipment certification for recycling of HFC-134a to meet the standard of purity.

4.2.4 SAE J1732—HFC-134a Extraction Equipment for Mobile Air Conditioning Systems—This covers equipment certification for removal of HFC-134a from mobile A/C systems that shall be sent off-site for process to meet the appropriate ARI 700 purity level.

4.2.5 SAE 1770—Automotive Refrigerant Recycle Equipment for Multiple Refrigerants—(R12/R134a) Equipment that recycle both R12 and R134a using common refrigerant circuits must meet the requirements of SAE J1770 to assure maximum allowable levels of cross contamination in the recycled refrigerants.

5. Purity of Refrigerant

5.1 SAE J1991—Standard of Purity for use in Mobile Air Conditioning Systems—This identifies the purity level of recycled R12 refrigerant after a contaminated sample has been processed in accordance with SAE J1990.

5.1.1 Purity of Recycled Refrigerant—SAE J1991 standard of purity states, "the refrigerant in this document shall have been directly removed from, and intended to be returned to, a mobile air conditioning system. Purity specification of reclaimed R12 refrigerant supplied in containers from other sources, for service of mobile air conditioning systems, shall meet ARI Standard 700-93."

5.1.2 With many other uses of CFC-12 it is important that the source of the refrigerant be known. Since CFC-12 is used in systems, such as refrigerators, water chillers, and central cooling systems, other contaminants and acids can be present.

5.1.3 Use of recycle equipment that meets SAE J1990 requirements may not purify the other used sources of CFC-12 to meet mobile air conditioning purity requirements.

5.1.4 CFC-12 from any source, other than a mobile air conditioning system, should not be used unless it has been returned to a reclamation facility that can return the purity to ARI 700-93 specification.

5.1.5 Use of refrigerant from other sources that contains acids and other contaminants, as well as a possible mixture of other refrigerants, will cause problems in mobile air conditioning systems.

5.2 SAE J2099—Standard of Purity for Recycled HFC-134a for use in Mobile Air Conditioning Systems—This identifies the purity level of recycled refrigerant after a contaminated sample has been processed in SAE J2210.

6. Technician Service Procedures

6.1 Two documents provide technician service procedures when servicing mobile air conditioning systems using R12 and R134a refrigerants.

6.2 SAE J1989—Recommended Service Procedure for Containment of R12—This document covers the technician refrigerant recovery procedure when servicing R12 mobile air conditioning systems and identification of excess NCGs.

6.3 SAE J2211—Recommended Service Procedure for Containment of HFC-134a—This document covers the technician refrigerant recovery procedure when servicing HFC-134a mobile air conditioning systems and identification of excess NCGs.

SAE J2219 Revised OCT94

7. System Service—The design of systems affects the amount of time required to extract all of the refrigerant prior to opening the system for repair.

7.1 Systems using an accumulator require special attention, additional time and precautions. When refrigerant is removed during extraction from accumulator systems, the low system pressure results in the accumulator becoming very cold with external frost sometimes being in evidence.

7.2 Since the accumulator contains both lubricant and refrigerant, a large quantity of refrigerant will remain in the system until the system has equalized. Until the accumulator reaches the temperature of the surrounding area it will continue to outgas refrigerant.

7.3 Since both the lubricant and refrigerant are at this condition, venting and safety are of concern. If the liquid refrigerant has not been completely removed and the refrigerant lines are opened, as the accumulator warms a sudden release of the mixture the can occur.

7.4 Use of external heat sources will raise the pressure in the accumulator and reduce the extraction time. **At no time should an open flame torch be used.**

7.5 All the refrigerant must be removed before opening any of the system refrigerant connections.

7.6 SAE J1989 and J2211 provide procedures to assure that the refrigerant has been extracted from the mobile air conditioning system.

8. Service Procedures—The SAE documents J1989 (R12) and J2211 (R134a) provide guidelines for containment and assurance that all the refrigerant has been removed from the system during service activity.

8.1 Refrigerant Containing Noncondensable Gases (Air)—If recycled refrigerant contains noncondensable gases (air) in excess of the allowable amount, high system operating pressure will occur, resulting in loss of performance and possible system damage.

8.2 Properly operating recycle equipment will remove excess air, provide the maximum level of allowable air in recycled refrigerant, and provide recycled refrigerant ready for use.

8.3 Verification for excess noncondensable contents in auxiliary portable containers of recycled refrigerant is important. Proper procedure to assure correct noncondensable level is outlined in SAE J1989 (R12) and SAE J2211 (R134a).

8.3.1 If the container contains excess air, as identified in the procedures in 8.3, it should be completely recycled.

NOTE—Only "DOT" refillable certified containers should be used.

9. System Lubricant Charge—It is important that system lubricant charge be maintained to assure proper system operation.

9.1 Component replacement should follow guidelines supplied by the manufacturer for lubricant addition during system service.

9.2 In general, recycle equipment will remove very little, if any, lubricant from the air conditioning system during the extraction operation. Design of refrigerant extraction/recycle equipment requires that the amount of lubricant removed during refrigerant removal be measured.

9.3 The removed lubricant must not be reused in the system. If air conditioning system lubricant addition is required only new lubricant, as specified by the manufacturer, should be added.

9.4 Used lubricant should be disposed of in accordance with local, state, and Federal laws.

9.5 Removal of a large quantity of lubricant during extraction may be an indication that the air conditioning system has been overcharged with lubricant.

9.6 Closed circuit power flushing to establish proper system lubricant level may be required. (SAE J1661)

9.7 If in doubt, refer to the system manufacturer service manual to assure proper lubricant charge.

9.8 If the measured lubricant sample, removed during the extraction operation, contains refrigerant dissolved in the lubricant, replacing this amount may result in replacement of excess new lubricant causing system overcharge.

10. *Service Activities* — When servicing the refrigerant system use of eye protection is required.

10.1 SAE J1629 — Cautionary Statements for Handling HFC-134a During Mobile Air Conditioning Service are identified.

10.1.1 Avoid breathing air conditioning refrigerant and lubricant vapor or mist. Exposure may irritate eyes, nose, and throat. **To remove HFC-134a from air conditioning system, use service equipment certified to meet the requirements of SAE J2210.**

10.1.2 Do not pressure test or leak test HFC-134a service equipment and/or vehicle air conditioning systems with compressed air. Some mixtures of air and HFC-134a have been shown to be combustible at elevated pressures. These mixtures, if ignited, may cause injury or property damage.

10.2 Service Tools — Service equipment including recycle equipment, hoses, and gauge manifolds must be used with only one refrigerant. Use of equipment on systems with different refrigerants will result in contamination caused from refrigerant and lubricant residue in the lines being charged directly to the system and equipment.

10.3 SAE J2196 — Service Hose for Automotive Air Conditioning — This defines service equipment (gauge lines), hose emission rates, hose construction requirements, and appropriate markings.

10.4 SAE J2197 — HFC-134a Service Hose Fittings for Automotive Air Conditioning Service Equipment

10.4.1 To prevent mixing of HFC-134a, with other refrigerants, an 1/2 in Acme thread fitting for containers was developed by the "Compressed Gas Association" (CGA) for small cans and 30 pound containers. This 1/2-in Acme thread is also required on HFC-134a automotive service equipment and a 14 mm hose fitting to prevent cross contamination between refrigerants.

10.5 Flushing of Systems — The past practice of open flushing systems with CFCs such as CFC-11 and CFC-12 can no longer be continued because Federal and local laws prohibit venting of CFCs to the atmosphere. For many years, R11 and R113 have been used for open vent flushing when cleaning mobile air conditioning systems. Technical information indicates that even small amounts of R11 residue will cause problems when used in conjunction with HFC-134a systems.

10.5.1 Methylchloroform (1,1,1 trichloroethane) is also covered by the Montreal Protocol phase-out and should not be considered for flushing.

10.5.2 Use of recycle equipment with adapters for closed loop power flushing of the system can provide containment, remove lubricant, and clean the refrigerant. Verify equipment capability with the manufacturer.

10.5.3 Due to small refrigerant passages within air conditioning system components (evaporator/condenser refrigerant circuits) flushing may not remove failed compressor material from some system components. Some A/C system manufacturers recommend that flushing not be considered after mechanical failure. The use of an in-line filter is considered the more effective method of containing the failed particles.

10.5.4 Use of other flushing solvents are areas of concern since, depending on the boiling point, the vacuum pump may not remove the solvent which will remain in the system, possibly affecting the chemical stability of the refrigerant for future use and the vehicle air conditioning system. In addition, safety concerns for flushing material that have low-flash temperatures can become flammable under normal conditions.

10.5.5 The use of flushing solvents, and procedures not approved by the air conditioning system manufacturer, may affect system seals and O-rings, remain in the system, and may result in future system failures.

10.5.6 To power flush a separate part or the complete system, the flushing equipment must be in series with the portion which is being flushed. Attaching to the system at the gauge service ports, even with the valve cores removed will not provide adequate system flushing. Using this method will result in the flushing being confined to the system's lowest pressure circuit and may not result in the removal of material.

10.5.7 Due to the complex air conditioning system chemical stability concerns SAE has not established documents for system flushing requirements, other than using the system refrigerant (R12 or R134a) as a flushing media.

NOTE—Use only specified equipment and refrigerant when servicing mobile air conditioning systems to prevent contamination. Do not use CFC-11 or CFC-12 for flushing HFC-134a systems.

11. Leak Detection Devices—To assure that serviced systems are returned to original design intent leakage specification, leak detection devices should be used. Proper use of leak detection equipment is important since leaks may occur in locations that are not directly visible to the technician.

11.1 Electronic Detectors—Some electronic leak detectors will only indicate when subjected to CFC-12 and will not indicate on HFC-134a. Newer design electronic detectors will provide leakage identification of both refrigerants. The detector manufacturer can verify the type of refrigerant that the unit will identify.

11.2 SAE J1627—Rating Criteria for Electronic Leak Detectors—This document establishes the criteria for electronic leak detectors to identify refrigerant leaks.

11.3 SAE J1628—Technician Procedure for Using Electronic Refrigerant Leak Detectors for Service of Mobile Air Conditioning Systems—This document provides guidelines for the technician when using an electronic leak detector in determining a system refrigerant leak.

11.4 Leaks can be identified when the system pressure is at least 50 psig. This system pressure can be achieved with a refrigerant charge in the range of 7 to 15% of the total system charge amount. The system does not require a complete charge for leak identification.

11.5 Proper use of the detector, as identified by the manufacturer, is important in determining the system leak.

11.5.1 To keep systems from chemical contamination, it is recommended that leak detection be done only with the refrigerant which is specified for the system. Use of "shop air" for leak detection introduces both air and moisture into the system. Use of other gases having higher pressures, such as nitrogen, can result in system damage (e.g., evaporator failure) and may contaminate the lubricant.

11.6 Trace Dyes—The chemical composition and amount of trace (leak) dyes when injected in mobile air conditioning systems may cause problems. Trace dyes cannot identify the degree of leakage, as compared to the requirements of electronic leak detection devices.

11.7 Leak dyes should not be added to any mobile air conditioning system unless the specific product has been approved by the "OEM" system manufacturer.

11.8 SAE guidelines for trace dyes are being developed.

12. General Service

12.1 Correct air conditioning system refrigerant charge amounts should be used when servicing to maintain proper system operation. Use of electronic and mechanical measurement devices dispensing refrigerant should periodically be checked. It should also be noted that some governmental agencies require certification of the equipment when selling products by weight or volume.

12.2 Refrigerant Handling/Identification to Prevent Cross Contamination

12.2.1 There is no "drop in" refrigerant for retrofitting existing CFC-12 systems approved to date by the air conditioning system manufacturers.

12.3 Refrigeration Identification—With "trademark" refrigerant products in the marketplace it is important that the refrigerant container be verified for containing the proper refrigerant (R12/R134a) prior to use in mobile air conditioning systems.

12.4 System Identification—Only two refrigerants, CFC-12 and HFC-134a, are considered acceptable by both the auto manufacturers and the EPA Significant New Alternatives Policy "SNAP" program for use in passenger and truck mobile air conditioning systems that have been specifically designed, or modified, for each refrigerant. To distinguish CFC-12 from HFC-134a, different system service fittings, labels, and refrigerant containers have been provided. (Some bus systems use HCFC-22 for the refrigerant charge.)

12.4.1 Other refrigerants have been identified as environmentally acceptable replacements for CFC-12 under the EPA Significant New Alternatives Policy "SNAP" rule. This "SNAP" listing identifies the acceptable chemical composition; however, the EPA "SNAP' program did not test these refrigerants for performance, operation, or durability in mobile air conditioning systems.

12.5 Requirements in SAE J639 establish service fittings for CFC-12 and HFC-134a mobile air conditioning systems. CFC-12 systems use screw threads and HFC-134a systems use a quick couple design. Additional requirements include a system label that list the type and amount of refrigerant, and the type of lubricant required.

12.6 Containers of HFC-134a, for automotive use, have a unique fitting or hose connection and a light blue color (PMS 2975) for identification.

12.7 To prevent system cross contamination, SAE J2196 and J2197 require fittings and markings identifying HFC-134a service hoses, recycle equipment, and service gauge manifolds.

13. Consequences of Cross-Contamination

13.1 Mixing of Refrigerants

13.2 Under no circumstance should refrigerants be mixed either in a system or in recovery/recycle equipment since it will affect recycle programs and may cause equipment and system damage.

13.2.1 Damage can include compressor failure, damage to recycle equipment, and transfer of the mixed refrigerant to other vehicles causing additional problems.

13.3 With two acceptable refrigerants in the service sector, it is important that CFC-12 and HFC-134a not be mixed in a system. Use of other refrigerants can cause additional system and service equipment problems.

13.3.1 Use of hydrocarbon refrigerants may result in safety concerns including system operation, service equipment, and the technician.

13.3.2 Refrigerants containing CFCs or HCFCs can not be vented and require specific recovery and recycle equipment. These hydrocarbon or blend combination refrigerants must meet SAE J1657 requirements.

13.4 If CFC-12 and HFC-134a are mixed in the same system, increased pressures of up to 25% can occur resulting in loss of performance and system damage.

13.5 It is essential that the service technician use only the OEM recommended refrigerant and service equipment to make sure refrigerant mixing does not occur.

13.6 Recycle equipment that has been contaminated will identify that the refrigerant container contains excess NCGs (air) due to the higher pressure of the mixed refrigerants. Equipment having automatic NCG purge may vent the entire tank due to this pressure. On manual systems, if indicated gauge pressure is higher than NCG value, the container should be considered as being contaminated refrigerant. Refrigerant contamination levels in the 2% to 5% range may indicate pressure readings in the same range as identification for NCGs.

13.7 Use of refrigerants other than identified for the system during "top off" service activities, which is not a recommended service procedure, will not improve system performance, and may cause system damage.

13.8 With the concern regarding contaminated mobile air conditioning systems and refrigerant supplies SAE developed J1771 "Refrigerant Identification" equipment requirements.

14. *Desiccant Failure*
—It has been determined that use of a new receiver/accumulator containing XH5 desiccant (originally used for R12 systems) breakdown may occur in an R134a refrigerant system, resulting in expensive system failure. When air conditionning system desiccant replacement is required XH7 or XH9 type or equivalent should be used for either R12 or R134a systems.

15. Lubricants

15.1 Current CFC-12 systems use mineral-based lubricants.

15.2 HFC-134a systems use several types of PAG lubricants and proper type and amount is important. The system label will identify the type of lubricant required.

SAE J2219 Revised OCT94

15.3 The compressors have been developed by each manufacturer to use a specific lubricant and use of other lubricants may affect compressor operation, durability, and warranty. Use only the lubricant specified by the manufacturer since mixing of PAG lubricants may also cause system problems.

15.4 Polyalkylene Glycol (PAG) lubricants absorb moisture so air conditioning systems, during servicing, and containers of new lubricant should be kept closed to reduce moisture entry.

15.5 Lubricants used in R134a systems should be handled with care to prevent skin contact by using impervious gloves. If skin contact should occur, wash the material off with plenty of soap and water.

15.6 Lubricant contact may also cause damage to painted surfaces, plastic parts, and other vehicle components.

15.7 Coating at installation of O-rings and seals with mineral oil can be done since this small amount will not affect the system. This will also reduce the possibility of connector corrosion due to the PAGs absorbed moisture.

16. Recommendations for Retrofitting CFC-12 Systems to a Non-CFC Refrigerant—The world auto air conditioning manufacturers have selected HFC-134a as the replacement refrigerant for new vehicles, and for retrofitting the CFC-12 fleet. It is recommended that CFC-12 systems continue using CFC-12 until it is no longer available. These systems were designed to operate with CFC-12 and the system manufacturers have considered the necessary system modifications to retrofit them to HFC-134a. The industry will provide information, where applicable, on retrofitting a CFC-12 vehicle to use HFC-134a.

16.1 The only source of information for use of replacement refrigerant is the original manufacturer of the mobile air conditioning system. In compliance with SAE J639, the type of refrigerant, amount, and manufacturer of the system should be indicated on the vehicle air conditioning system.

17. Fittings and Labels

17.1 SAE Standard J1660 established service fittings and labels to identify conversion of CFC-12 systems to use HFC-134a. New unique system service access fittings are required for other replacement refrigerants to prevent equipment and refrigerant contamination.

17.2 The EPA has included these fittings and label requirements in rule making for the retrofitting of the CFC-12 fleet.

18. Retrofitting Mobile Air Conditioning Systems With Replacement Refrigerants

18.1 Documents were developed at the request of EPA to identify alternate refrigerants and retrofit procedures for conversion of CFC-12 mobile air conditioning systems.

18.2 SAE J1657—Selection Criteria for Retrofit Refrigerants to Replace R12 in Mobile Air Conditioning Systems

18.3 The purpose is to provide criteria for determining acceptability of candidate retrofit refrigerants to replace R12 in mobile air conditioning systems. This includes flammability, ozone depletion, toxicity and other refrigerant and lubricant compatibility requirements to be usable in mobile A/C systems.

19. Blend Refrigerants Containing HCFC

19.1 Mixing of refrigerant blends with CFC-12 or HFC-134a may cause problems which could result in system failure.

SAE J2219 Revised OCT94

19.2 Do not modify any CFC-12 system to use a refrigerant blend unless modification procedures are supplied by the original system manufacturer.

19.3 The Clean Air Act requires that any refrigerant containing HCFC, must comply with Section 609 effective January 1, 1992, which includes non-venting during service and recycling.

20. *SAE J1658—Alternate Refrigerant Consistency Criteria for Use in Mobile Air Conditioning Systems*

20.1 Blend refrigerants consist of more than one substance, this document identifies the proper handling procedure, vapor or liquid phase, and identifies when the remaining container contents cannot be used due to improper blend consistency.

21. *SAE J1659—Vehicle Testing Requirements for Replacement Refrigerants for use in R12 Mobile Air Conditioning Systems*

21.1 This requires certain vehicle tests which must be conducted to establish any system performance changes due to the alternate refrigerant.

22. *SAE J1662—Material Compatibility With Alternate Refrigerants*

22.1 Seals, hoses, and O-rings used in CFC-12 systems may not be compatible with some alternate refrigerants and could break down causing system failures. This document covers test procedures for establishing material compatibility.

23. *Conversion from CFC-12 to HFC-134a*

NOTE—Do not directly use HFC-134a in CFC-12 systems.

23.1 Retrofit procedures supplied by the original system manufacturer should be followed before modifying CFC-12 systems to use HFC-134a.

23.2 Mixing of HFC-134a with CFC-12 without proper retrofit of system components may cause problems which could result in system failure.

24. *SAE J1660—Fittings and Labels for Retrofit or R12 Mobile Air Conditioning Systems to R134a*

24.1 This document covers modification of service fittings and labels for retrofitted vehicles to prevent future system damage and contamination of refrigerant supplies.

24.2 SAE J1661—Procedure for Retrofitting R12 Mobile Air Conditioning Systems to R134a

24.2.1 This covers the retrofit modification and system processing procedure to reduce the remaining system R12 residue to less than 2%, which is required to reduce future contamination of the R134a refrigerant supply when the vehicle is serviced.

25. *Modifications for Alternate Refrigerant*

25.1 System modifications depending on vehicle model required to retrofit CFC-12 systems may include hose, high-pressure cut out device, seals, desiccant, lubricant, refrigerant control replacement, increased condenser capacity, and other modifications as determined by the equipment manufacturer. Not following the "OEM" recommendation may result in system damage, loss of performance, and affect warranty.

25.2 Do not use any refrigerant other than the one specified for the system unless the manufacturer has supplied information for conversion.

25.3 If a conversion (retrofit) program is provided by the system manufacturer, perform the complete required conversion. Partial conversion may result in problems which can include loss of performance, system failure, and possibly void warranty.

25.4 Areas of Concern—Use of improper refrigerant can result in many problems:

   a. Leakage of hose and seals
   b. Damage to desiccant material
   c. Cause system refrigerant control problems
   d. Cause compressor problems including failure
   e. Compressor failure due to wrong lubricant
   f. Loss of system performance due to evaporator control for freeze protection and expansion valve calibration
   g. Higher system operating pressure resulting in reduced performance, and possible failures

25.5 Use of flammable refrigerants add additional safety concerns since the vehicle air conditioning system and service equipment are not designed for its use. Use of flammable refrigerants in mobile air conditioning systems are prohibited in some states.

25.6 SAE J639 identifies that refrigerant used in mobile air conditioning systems be low toxicity and nonflammable. In addition, several states have specific regulation identifying these requirements.

26. Notes

26.1 Marginal Indicia—The (R) is for the convenience of the user in locating areas where technical revisions have been made to the previous issue of the report. If the symbol is next to the title, it indicates a complete revision of the document.

PREPARED BY THE SAE INTERIOR CLIMATE CONTROL STANDARDS COMMITTEE

Appendix B

Federal Certification and Record-Keeping Requirements

(Excerpted from the final rule of 40 CFR, Part 82)

(a) *Certification requirements*

(1.) No later than January 1, 1993, all persons repairing or servicing motor vehicle air conditioners for consideration shall certify to the Administrator that such person has acquired and is properly using approved equipment and that each individual authorized to use the equipment is properly trained and certified. The data elements for certification are as follows:

[i] The name of the purchaser of the equipment,
[ii] The address of the establishment where the equipment will be located,
[iii] The manufacturer name and model number, and date of manufacture, and the serial number of the equipment,
[iv] The owner of the equipment or another responsible officer must sign the certification stating that the equipment will be properly used in servicing vehicle air conditioners, that each individual authorized by the purchaser to perform service is properly trained and certified in accordance with [40 CFR Part] §82.40, and that the information given is true and correct. The certification should be sent to:

> MVACs Recycling Program Manager
> Stratospheric Ozone Protection Branch
> (6202-J)
> US Environmental Protection Agency
> 401 M Street, SW
> Washington, DC 20460

(2.) No later than January 1, 1992, persons repairing or servicing vehicle air conditioners for consideration at an entity which performed service on fewer than 100 motor vehicle air conditioners in calendar year 1990 must so certify to the Administrator unless they acquire and properly use approved refrigerant recycling equipment under [40 CFR Part]§82.36. Persons must retain adequate records to demonstrate that the number of vehicles serviced was fewer than 100.

(3.) Certificates of compliance are not transferable. In the event of a change of ownership of an entity which services motor vehicle air conditioners for consideration, the new owner of the entity shall certify within thirty days of the change of ownership pursuant to [40 CFR Part] §82.44(1)[a].

(4.) Any person who owns approved recycling equipment certified under §82.36(a)(2) must maintain records of the name and address of any facility to which refrigerant is sent.

(5.) Any person who owns approved recycle equipment must maintain records demonstrating that all persons authorized to operate the equipment are currently certified under [40 CFR Part] §82.40.

(6.) Any person who sells or distributes any class I or class II substance that is suitable for use as a refrigerant in a motor vehicle air conditioner and is in a container of less than 20 pounds must verify that the purchaser is properly trained and certified under [40 CFR Part] ¤ 82.40.

(7.) Any person who conducts any retail sale of class I or class II substance that is suitable for use as a refrigerant in a motor vehicle air conditioner and is in a container of less than 20 pounds must prominently display a sign which states: It is a violation of federal law to sell containers of Class I and Class II refrigerant of less than 20 pounds to anyone who is not properly trained and certified to operate approved refrigerant recycling equipment.

(8.) All records required to be maintained pursuant to this section must be kept for a minimum of three years unless otherwise indicated. Entities which service motor vehicle air conditioners for consideration must keep these records on-site.

(9.) All entities which service motor vehicle air conditioners for consideration must allow an authorized representative of the administrator entry onto their premises (upon presentation of his or her credentials) and give the authorized representative access to all records required to be maintained pursuant to this section.

```
                    YOURA    R
                             629
                             .277
                             G685
                             2ED
GOTT, PHILIP G.
    AUTOMOTIVE AIR-CONDI-
TIONING REFRIGERANT SER-
VICE GUIDE    PAPER
```

2/17/99 $25.00